Playing for Keeps

Playing for Keeps

LIFE AND LEARNING
ON A PUBLIC SCHOOL PLAYGROUND

Deborah Meier, Brenda S. Engel, and Beth Taylor

Teachers College, Columbia University
New York and London

Published by Teachers College Press, 1234 Amsterdam Avenue, New York, NY 10027

Library of Congress Cataloging-in-Publication Data

Meier, Deborah.
  Playing for keeps : life and learning on a public school playground / Deborah Meier, Brenda S. Engel, and Beth Taylor.
       p.   cm.
  Includes bibliographical references and index.
  ISBN 978-0-8077-5095-7 (pbk : alk. paper)
  1. Mission Hill School (Boston, Mass.)   2. Playgrounds—Massachusetts—Boston.
3. Play—Social aspects—Massachusetts—Boston.   4. Child development—Massachusetts—Boston.   I. Engel, Brenda S.   II. Taylor, Beth.   III. Title.

  LD7501.B6M45 2010
  372.9744'61—dc22

                                                                2010009482

ISBN 978-0-8077-5095-7 (paper)

Printed on acid-free paper
Manufactured in the United States of America

17   16   15   14   13   12   11   10   1   2   3   4   5   6   7   8

There was a child went forth every day,
And the first object he looked upon, that object he became,
And that object became part of him for the day or a certain
    part of the day,
Or for many years or stretching cycles of years.
                —Walt Whitman, "There was a Child Went Forth"

We can turn into anything—water or fire, rain, thunder—not
shoes or paper or things like that.
                —Quote from a child, *Mission Hill School News*

Contents

Preface

One day, during recess, on the playground of the Mission Hill School, three 5-year-olds called to Beth (one of the authors of this book) to come over and see what they had found: some dried fungus on the beech tree. Their description: "It's hard." "It's growing bigger on the tree." "It's going on a circle." "It is dark colors, five colors." "It has white." And, finally, somewhat peremptorily, "Write it down," which she did. The children knew she would, anticipating with confidence her interest both in the fungus itself and in their observations of it.

This scene took place on the playground of the Mission Hill School, a few years after a seminal moment: Deborah Meier (having just retired from 30 years in the New York City public schools) drove up from New York City and, arriving at Brenda Engel's house in Cambridge, burst into the kitchen with an idea: "Why don't I move up here and we start an elementary school in Boston?" Excited by the thought, they called Eleanor Duckworth and Vito Perrone (both friends and prominent members of the faculty of the Harvard Graduate School of Education), who enthusiastically supported the prospect of a new school. And, as it turned out, it was a wonderful and wholly practicable idea.

The school Deborah Meier envisioned would be similar to Central Park East, the highly successful public school she had started on the Upper East Side of Manhattan. Central Park East and the associated network of schools subsequently founded by Meier in New York City in the 1970s and 1980s were based on old progressive educational ideas explored and brought up to date in a contemporary setting. The new school in Boston would embody many of the same ideas and, similarly, be part of the nationwide Coalition of Essential Schools (an association of progressive schools).

At the time of the meeting in Brenda's kitchen, a network of "pilot schools" was, fortuitously, being launched in the Boston public school (BPS) system, intended to explore ways of providing schools with charter-like flexibility within the Boston district. Meier assembled a planning committee of local educators (including co-author Beth Taylor) to work out the structural details of the proposed new school. The committee met over the winter of 1996–1997, and a successful application was then made to the BPS. The Mission Hill School opened its doors in the fall of 1997.

Deborah Meier became the school's first principal. Beth (then Lerman) Taylor and Brenda Engel (a volunteer) worked at the school from the start, with both children and staff. In addition to her regular presence on the playground at recess time, Beth tutored children singly and in groups, worked with teachers, and, for a period, actually took over teaching a fifth-grade class when a teacher left unexpectedly. Brenda, as well as tutoring children, developed academic evaluation systems for the school, initiated an archive of children's work, and pinch-hit wherever there was a need.

This book, grounded in Beth's observations recorded in her weekly column in the school newsletter, makes a case for the importance of free exploration, wonder, imagination, and play to the learning and growth of children. The observations allow the reader direct, unmediated access to children's words and activities during school hours outside the classrooms, in an unstructured, relatively natural environment. We, the authors, comment on the reported playground events in the light of our own experiences and understanding. By staying close to the observed scene, however, we try to avoid overanalysis of children's behavior, the interposition of adult theories and frameworks or speculation about social/cultural norms and pathologies.

We invite readers to appreciate the life of the imagination on the playground, to see the energy children bring to exploring their social and physical surrounds, and to share with us the children's delight in active learning. The book might even trigger for readers echoes of their own childhood experiences in the outdoors. We hope, of course, that through the descriptions and comments, readers will gain understanding of the importance of play in the lives of children.

None of us works at the school regularly anymore, but the school is still there. What is described in the following pages is essentially also still there, though in altered form: Most of the children and some of the teachers have changed; the playground, the subject of this book, has been "improved." But what meets the eyes and ears of the observer on the playground is still true to the original vision of the Mission Hill School.

All children's names are pseudonyms.

Acknowledgments

We want to acknowledge the many thoughtful, committed individuals responsible for the Mission Hill School becoming an extraordinarily joyful place to work and play—children, families and school staff, past and present.

Ayla Gavins, in particular, deserves recognition for successfully taking over as principal of the school in its ninth year. Ayla's experience as a teacher, her deep understanding and appreciation of children and how they learn, have enabled her to carry on and strengthen the school's progressive tradition.

Others contributed in various significant ways to the content of this book:

Marla Gaines, the school's administrative coordinator, helped us by retrieving the relevant names, dates, and facts having to do with the school's life for over a dozen years.

Caroline Hoppin, the energetic organizer and custodian of the Archives of Children's Work, assisted in identifying examples of children's work to further illustrate and amplify what we were writing about.

Joyce Stevens, a part-time staff member, is virtually a prototype of engaged, imaginative thinking (a central theme in the book). She read over parts of the text in draft and provided information, corrections, and suggestions.

Lukas Best, an eyewitness on the playground as a member of the staff, added to our information about the children and their recess activities.

Emily Gasoi (former second/third-grade teacher) and her students Brigitta Rachko, Selina Ruiz, and Bryanna Bedford recalled for us, 8 years later, some of the rhymes they had chanted for jump rope and clapping games.

Ann Ruggiero's sixth-grade students figured the angles and measurements of the school playground and carefully mapped it for this book. (Their map was then "backdated" by Beth Taylor to indicate the actual arrangements of the playground in 1998–2001.)

Jane Andrias, who was the art teacher, then director of Central Park East School in New York City for many years, was always available to look and listen whenever there was a need. She gave the benefit of her experience and wisdom to both the school and, personally, to Deborah Meier, its principal.

In a broader context, we also want to express our gratitude to several "tutelary spirits" who have been important to our thinking: Lillian Weber, whose writings were few but whose influence on a generation of elementary school reformers was immense; Patricia Carini, who taught us all the fine art of observation and its significance for educating the whole child; Vito Perrone, who made everything possible (including the Mission Hill School); Michael Armstrong, who, as a writer, teacher, and school head, always lived by his belief in the centrality of the imagination to education; and Eleanor Duckworth, a valued personal and professional friend to the authors and to the Mission Hill School from its very beginning.

Then, of course, there are the children; the children are the life of this story.

Note on Authorship

We all read, commented on, added to, and subtracted from one another's writings. We are jointly responsible for the Preface, Introduction, and Appendix. Chapter 6 and the "Holes and Rocks" section in Chapter 3 were written collaboratively by Brenda and Beth. Chapter 5 was written collaboratively by Deborah and Brenda. The Epilogue is by Deborah. All the selections from the columns quoted in the text were written by Beth. Brenda wrote the commentaries in Chapters 1, 2, 3, 4, 7, 8, and 9; she also organized and edited the book's contents.

Playing for Keeps

Introduction

THE SCHOOL: SETTING

The school is on Mission Hill in Roxbury, a neighborhood of Boston. The building is located a few steep blocks up from Tremont Street, one of the area's main commercial thoroughfares. Twice a day, yellow school buses make their way laboriously up the incline of Parker Street and stop at the corner of the dead-end side street fronting the school to unload their passengers. The process is reversed in the afternoon when school gets out.

The school itself occupies one and a half floors of a large, imposing, three-story building, formerly a Catholic high school. The architecture is traditional 1920s school style, and the building itself, of tawny-brown brick, clearly conveys its serious function—to contain and educate youth. The classrooms and administrative office are on the second floor, opening onto a 14-foot-wide corridor that serves as common space for the display of student work and other materials of general interest as well as for small-group activities. The outdoor play space is behind and to the left of the building.

"NOTES FROM OUTDOORS"

The school published (and still publishes) a weekly four-page newsletter for parents and friends of the school, with a calendar, notices of events, classroom observations, and a weekly column usually written by Deborah Meier. Beth Taylor, after having regularly made notes on what she observed while out on the playground with the children during recess, began writing a column, "Notes from Outdoors," for the newsletter based on these notes. The columns conveyed in vivid detail the children's lives on the playground—their imaginative play and games; their wonderings and discoveries about nature; their social relationships, physical feats, and competitions. Beth's faithful transcriptions of the children's words along with the descriptions of the activities brought the readers new insights into the world of play and new appreciation of its physical, emotional, and intellectual value.

Mission Hill School.

The columns became, for adults and children, a popular item, read consistently each week by the school community. We soon realized that, in its low-key, informal style, Beth's columns were carrying the load for us all, expressing our viewpoint about learning. When Beth finally left Mission Hill years later, the absence of that column was conspicuous; it was acutely missed by the whole school community.

Deborah Meier recognized and valued the unique quality and content of these writings from the years 1998–2001. The columns clearly demonstrated children's ability to create imaginary worlds, sometimes reflective of adult lives, sometimes of their own often mysterious interests, concerns, preoccupations, and desires. The question was what to do with them. Simply reprinting the columns out of context would lack meaning. Brenda Engel, equally enthusiastic about the columns when they appeared, came up with an idea: to make selections from the columns centering on emergent themes in the children's play, the selections to be preceded by a brief explanation and followed by comments and further thoughts. This then became the basic scheme of this book.

In the face of the current attack on the world of play and childhood, we saw this as an opportunity to reassert our convictions about the value of play—its meaning to growth, education, and life in a democratic society. At the core of the book are Beth's reports from a realm we might foolishly allow to disappear.

THE PLAYGROUND

There were several distinctive features of the Mission Hill School playground that gave each area a particular character. These features, natural or human-made, suggested possibilities for activities: the tree, the walls, and the hardtop. Children chose where to play according to the individual's or group's inclinations, often returning to the same area to continue a game from a previous recess time. The playground was a landscape to which the children responded, taking advantage of what they found and transforming it according to their imaginative needs.

The beech tree was dead and stood close to the chain-link fence that separated the school land from a convent next door. The tree was as tall as the three-story school building and had limbs that stretched out and up. It had not been dead long, and the bark was still firm and smooth. It had probably died, said an arborist, because it was on a slope and a very hot, dry summer had robbed its shallow roots of moisture. Six children could hold hands around its trunk, just. The land on which it stood sloped from the street to the walkway, and there was tall unkempt grass growing around it. The city agreed to take the tree down—to cut it about 6 feet above the roots and let the branches fall where they might. As they sawed the tree, children looked out of the windows and saw the heavy trunk fall. The men then cut off the smaller branches and chopped them into wood chips, which they spread around the tree. No part of the tree was taken away.

Children, six to eight years old, on trunk of felled beech tree.

The trunk lying on the ground, with the more substantial limbs still attached, had spaces under it where children could sit. The trunk had indentations along it, "like an elephant's skin," said a child. The limbs were smooth. The remaining part, the stump, stood up straight beside the cut part, its roots spreading out into the grass. The children counted over 100 rings on the sawed-off end of the trunk, looked at the different spacing between the rings, and talked about what might have caused some circles to be closer together.

The tree soon became the place to which many children of different ages ran when they came out after lunch. Over the 4 years, the standing trunk and the horizontal section with its branches became a laboratory for observation and exploration of the natural world; it served as a gym for climbing and jumping; and it was a prop that inspired imaginative scenes and games.

There were four important walls that became the focus for much of the children's play and explorations. The wall that separated the school from neighboring houses was about 12 feet high, made of a yellowish brick with a capping of slanted brick at the top. It extended the whole length of the school property down to the street at the end. It was used as a backboard for ball games—throwing and catching large and small balls,

Friends, five and six years old, near wall of grassy area.

kickball, tennis, and street hockey—and the space next to it was where the snowplow left piles of snow. The part that bordered the upper level of the play area was shadowed by Norway maples and other smaller trees. It was damp and shady there most of the year. Small ferns and moss grew out from the crevices in the mortar. Leaves piled up at the base of the wall, and weeds and grass grew on the grass behind the leaves.

The first few days the children were in school, they explored the walls. There were screams of excitement and fear as they found snails among the ferns, salamanders in the damp leaves, and garter snakes slithering in the grass. The grassy part of the play area was separated from the hardtop by a retaining wall about 3 feet high. This wall also served as a boundary for ball games and other activities on the hardtop. It was a place where children sat to talk and to practice jumping, climbing, and balancing.

The cement path that led from the school ended at the gate of the chain-link fence. Both sides of this path were framed by a low wall. At the three sets of steps, the wall was high enough to become a favorite place for "cooking," "riding motorcycles," telling stories, and planning activities. It had postholes that collected water and became pots for mixing mud pies and leaf soups. It served, as well, as the support for fairy houses of leaves and sticks and moss. It was also dangerous. When children tried

Seven-year-olds playing Three Billy Goats Gruff.

to run and jump across the path and walls in one leap, they could catch a foot and fall, skinning a hand or leg.

The fourth wall that added to the varied environment was the wall of the school itself, which was three stories high and had four low window-sills. The building shaded this part of the sloping grassy area and made a cool space in the hot days and kept the snow from melting in the winter. Ice often formed in the lowest area, which again was dangerous but also provided a wonderful place to test what ice was like.

When the grassy areas were wet or muddy, they were closed and children of all ages played on the hardtop. Double doors from the school building opened onto a set of wide steps leading down to the hardtop. The hardtop extended half a football field's length behind the school building to the fence along the street. It was used after school by the neighborhood. Except for the end near the parking lot and street, which was set aside for basketball, it was nearly always shady. It was resurfaced during the first year of the school, and a large oval track was painted on it alongside a map of the United States, some courts marked for the game four square, and a large compass. At one place on the back wall of the school there was an old coal bunker, an enclosed place with no roof. A high brick wall along the east side separated the school from the neighboring

Mission Hill School

PLAY GROUND 1998-2001

Map of Playground as it was in 1998–2001.

houses. Basketball began in a very small way with portable hoops; when they were broken, a fence was built and permanent hoops installed.

The majority of older children (11 to 13) played on the hardtop all year long, but there were always a few playing with younger children on the grassy areas, or taking notes about their play (probably in imitation of Beth), or talking with the teacher. Sometimes they went to the tree to sit and talk or sunbathe. Sometimes they used the empty coal bunker for talking and for refuge during imaginative games when the grassy areas were too icy or muddy to play on. Ordinary tag and freeze tag were popular at various times. The walls of the school and doorway became "safe havens" during chasing games.

The stories and games—both newly invented and as familiar as old myths and folk tales—took place in all the areas of the playground. The characters, props, settings, plots, and rules varied, but the underlying themes reflect the durable, challenging, and important issues in the lives of schoolchildren.

THE CHILDREN

Who, then, were the children who, in the spaces outside the school walls, ran, jumped, dug, laughed, pretended, quarreled, sat, climbed, reflected,

I'm 5 1/2 years old and big sister to Maya. I enjoy ballet, soccer and Flamenco dancing. Oh yeah, I love J.P. Licks and of course meeting new friends.

My daddy grew up in Boston, but later moved to Virginia where he met my mommy and later they married and moved to Boston. I have lived in Boston all my life - although I spend <u>alot</u> of time in Virginia with Nana. Once while I was visiting I saw a real live bear!

We chose the Mission Hill School because it's a neighborhood school dedicated to creating education where parents, teachers and community take part in my future. I want to be a dancer and a doctor.

Kindergartner's autobiography dictated to teacher.

constructed, and talked? Who were the children who, those days, played games and imagined themselves into other roles and other places? They were ordinary (if children are ever ordinary) urban children, ages 5 through 14 (by year 3 of the school), self-selected only to the extent that their parents had chosen for them this particular, rather adventurous educational setting: a Boston "pilot school" designed to embody the progressive ideas of its founder, Deborah Meier. They were a diverse group—from different ethnic, cultural, and economic backgrounds, living in different areas of Boston.

Years later, when we sat down to recall the children in the school during those early years, a small group of large, strong, managerial older girls came immediately and vividly to mind, a group that, in spite of occasional quarrels, generally "hung out" together. They exercised their authority by organizing the younger children (recess included children of a range of ages)—laying out "rules," teaching them to jump rope and recite the accompanying chants, and lining them up in "parades." One of these older girls had an impressively large repertoire of jump-rope rhymes that she willingly taught to the others.

At times this group of girls acted as somewhat overaffectionate guardians—hugging, kissing, almost stifling the smaller ones to the point where some of the latter actively rebelled. A conspicuous presence on the

FRINDS
FRINDS
I LIKE
FRINDS
AND I HAVE
A LOT. AND
WHAR AVAR
I GO I SEE
FRINDS

"Friends": Poem by eight-year-old.

playground, these borderline teens expressed an uncertain sense of themselves as more sophisticated, strolling about, appearing somewhat "above it all"; then, forgetting, they would become enthusiastically involved in games with the others.

In the meantime, many of their classmates were engaged in various more structured activities with balls—soccer, football, or basketball, depending on the season. Girls also claimed equal rights—to play basketball, even football.

The kindergartners, when they first experienced the playground, tended to stay safely in the grassy areas, playing among themselves, not yet daring to venture into the larger, more open spaces populated by older students. After a few weeks, after gaining confidence, they drifted over and became part of the general activities.

We remembered, too, a group of second- and third-grade boys and girls who rushed madly around the playground, challenging and yelling to each other, performing feats of daring and strength and often disrupting quieter activities. Because of safety considerations, these "high-energy" characters sometimes needed to be stopped in midflight by a teacher. When they became interested in a "project" like building or digging, they could be focused and collaborative.

Boys and girls of all ages were involved in imaginative play in various areas of the playground, some characteristically as initiators (often the older children), others as followers—though these roles could and did change.

There were always two or three "serious" children who wanted to hang out and talk with the adults, commenting on the behavior of the younger ones or initiating a discussion of books they had been reading or movies seen. In warmer weather, some actually brought books outside and found a comfortable spot on the wall, on the steps, or under a bush, to spend recess reading. Inspired by Beth's example, a few girls too began to bring pads and pencils and make notes.

Finally, there were several children who had serious difficulties managing themselves on the playground—as they did also in the classrooms. The supervising adults needed to be especially aware of these individuals in order to avoid catastrophic behavior—fights, rock throwing, sudden violent attacks, and so forth. With attention and support from the staff, most of these children made dramatic progress in the course of time, becoming happier and easier with other children.

While students' and parents' satisfaction with the school and its "playful" approach remained high, some families, especially of children in the upper grades, chose to transfer their kids to more traditional, selective schools or, in a few cases, to schools that they thought were equipped to attend to their children's particular needs.

Sources of Play

Parents, teachers, and other observers of children often wonder, "How did that idea ever get into her head?" or "Where in the world did he learn about that?" or even "I never knew she was listening!" You can never tell about children: Things are going on in their heads during all their waking (and possibly sleeping) hours, much of which would be surprising to adults. Some of their thoughts and feelings see the light of day on the playground, expressed and represented in various ways.

At times the inspiration behind the playground dramas is obvious— life at home, for example, or TV, or the school curriculum. The origins of some, however, seem far-fetched or mysterious, their sources multiple or unclear. All the primary material, however, no matter what its inspiration, becomes significantly transformed through children's imaginations. Disparate elements are joined together, the magical and the realistic seamlessly interwoven.

Each of the four chapters in Part I focuses on one general thematic area of play; the chapters are then subdivided into topics with more particular content. Chapter 1 concerns families—where and how they live as well as the relationships among family members (including members of animal families). Chapter 2 describes the various ways in which children act out ideas and reenact events that frighten them. Chapter 3 shows children exploring the natural environment of the playground, and, in Chapter 4, dramatizing ideas from the school curriculum.

The quoted excerpts from Beth's columns in "News from Outdoors," are, accordingly, organized thematically rather than chronologically. The excerpts give immediacy to the playground scenes, bringing the reader close to the action. The experienced reader (and we've all experienced childhood) will recognize the authenticity of these reports "from the field." Our, the authors', comments following the excerpts reflect our thinking about the playground events as defining experiences of childhood.

⬿ 1 ⬾

Domesticity

HOUSES AND CASTLES

One day a child got to the tree and sat astride the highest part. "Welcome to my home," she said, as the others reached the tree.

On another day a child pointed to parts of the branches she was astride and said, "This is a pool. This is my sissy. That is my dog."

Four 11- and 12-year-olds ran to the tree, climbed on it and jumped from it: "I didn't know this was here. It is wonderful."

At the beech tree there have been many houses, sometimes two or three at a time.

According to the common childhood wisdom, families live in houses. Regardless of the fact that many of the city-dwelling children at the Mission Hill School live in apartments, in space shared with relatives or even, occasionally, in shelters, the image of the one-family house persists in their play. (Urban children, in fact, when asked to draw houses, typically draw them with a center-front door, a window to either side, a pitched roof, and often a row of tulips or grass along the bottom. Even children who live in apartment complexes and have rarely seen a free-standing house of this description continue to paint or draw the familiar, emblematic version.)

The "idea" of house, its meaning to children, seems to have little to do with the reality of their daily experience, more to do with a focus for values like family, food, warmth, safety, and protection. In their house play, children act out these values.

On the Mission Hill School playground where there were no proper building materials; the children had to improvise, to vary and extend their concept of "house." The horizontal beech tree provided the basic structure for many dwellings, as did the spaces under the lilac bushes. To an outsider, some of these structures would have been hard to recognize

Seven-year-old's drawing of her community.

as houses though they accommodated the most important features of "home"—a protected place (preferably with a roof, something resembling walls, and a front door) in which to cook meals and go to sleep. Most were equipped with approximations of a stove, beds, and other furniture. Significantly, however, the houses did not always turn out to be safe. They were vulnerable to fires, robbers, and wolves among other hazards.

> Houses were built with logs, grass, and bark around the base of the tree. "We just moved in," said Ellie. She pointed to a nest of grass. "It's the chair."

> "I'll lock the doors."

> "You have to be careful as you play," observed one child, "because you won't be able to hear predators from the front."

Seven- and eight-year-olds building ramp to beech tree.

The tree became a castle one day: "Do you want to be the princess?" "I'm the guard. Go get your father and tell him it's bedtime."

The tree also has secret powers and is sometimes a car, a horse, a place to practice jumping, or the safe place for the "good guys."

Twelve children of mixed ages have been playing a family game with crying babies, a volcano, burning houses, and tornadoes.

The boys went on for the entire playtime, running and climbing as members of a family on a spaceship.

One group made a house in the corner for a mother bunny and her babies. A fox and, another day, a wolf came to scare them.

The words themselves, *house* and *home*, convey feelings of safety and security, places of refuge from the dangers and stresses of the outside world, places to go back to, forgiving places where you're accepted, where you "belong." Homes are popularly pictured as warm and cozy; on the playground they are mainly associated with food, sleep, and other domestic routines. This comforting view of home is idealized and differs from the children's actual experience: Homes in real life can be stressful scenes of tension, struggle, and unhappiness, with families in conflict or fragmented. In their play worlds, however, children can have it the way they want it; they can live in orderly, safe, conventional houses in proper families. Though the positive, wished-for, romantic images of domestic life on the whole dominate family play, less cheerful possibilities are woven in, perhaps as a concession to reality, perhaps as dramatic contrast.

Castles are upscale houses for royal families, further from the children's experience and, like forts, particularly safe. Few of the children have seen castles, the images coming from books, films, and TV. Spaceships, even more remote from experience, can also become homes for families.

The horizontal trunk and stretching branches of the beech tree, occupying some 15 feet or so to the left of the school building, were natural forms, large and irregular. Because the tree was a distinctive place with no designated function, it lent itself to a variety of possibilities: It became a house, multiple houses, or a castle, perhaps because its spreading branches suggest protection, though it could also be a horse, a ship, a dinosaur, or a spaceship. Up in its branches the children could feel safe, at home, guarded by magic powers, unassailable. The tree's aura of protection extended to the area around the base.

Other places, particularly under the lilac bushes, also served as houses. The bushes offered seclusion, privacy, and something resembling a roof, all of these important attributes of house-as-home.

Outside the safety of houses there were many dangers: among others, tornadoes, storms, and volcanoes. Sometimes, even inside, scary, traumatic events took place: sick babies, fires, invading foxes and wolves. In a way these violent events emphasize, by contrast, the protection houses are meant to provide even when they fail to.

HOUSEKEEPING

Standards for responsible housekeeping, perhaps drummed in at home, were strictly and unquestioningly adhered to—in play if not always in real life: cleanliness, good food, schedules, and promptness.

> One day the tree was home to a large family with nine children. One child was lying on the ground. I [Beth] went over to see what had happened: "She's only three weeks old. It's nap time." A few seconds later, Juanita, the mother, called out: "It's time to eat

snack." The children sat on the tree to "eat." "It's time for church. Get your suits on, your jackets, your shoes," said Juanita. The children climbed down. "Follow me," said Juanita. "Walk straight to the church." The children quietly lined up and Juanita led them up the hill and across the steps to the lilac trees. On the way, an imaginary car nearly hit one of the children.

Some of the members of this group of 10 children played families in storms the previous week. They were joined by new children last week.

The sun is warm on the front hill where meals are being cooked: "We are making pork chops," Donna announces. "We're having a good dinner," says Kenya, adding, "I'm taking off the burnt parts. We're having a cookout and all our friends are coming over." Katie comes around the tree and says, "I'm a fairy." "Would you like some pork chops, little fairy?" "Thank you," says Katie. "What is this?" she asks, regarding the mixture of bark and dirt. "Pork chops," say the two cooks.

Every day a group of children ages five to nine play house along the side of the school. They bake pies and offer everyone a piece.

Mud continues to fascinate the children. "Look what I made—chocolate homemade stew," said Ari as he stirred the post hole with a stick.

Family games continue. I was invited to come to the lilac trees: "Come into our warm house. We are cooking chicken and you can have some."

Children "cook" in the post holes on the wall: "Here's a pizza I made for you—pepperoni, sausages, and a little bit of cheese," said a child as she handed me a large leaf with mud on it. A five year old brushed water and mud on maple leaves with sticks: "This is a chocolate chip cookie. The grass is the sparkles and the mud is the chocolate chips."

Another group raked and swept the lilac tree house. They were indignant when someone "brought dirt in the home after we cleaned it." "We vacuumed the floor," said Mira, using twigs to sweep. The next day more children were cleaning "the floor."

At the lilacs, a child said, "We'd better take care of my sister and make the house clean. I have to go to school."

"Sister, you know it is your birthday." "We should have a celebration today."

"Did you know there is a celebration today?" "Where will it be?" "It's going to be a tree party."

Lots and lots of food was prepared on the playground, most of it familiar home cooking like pies, pork chops, chicken, pizzas and some less common like "chocolate homemade stew." For raw materials, the children used whatever came to hand—bark, dirt, leaves, grass, mud. It is notable that the cooking activity was primarily social and communal: People usually cooked together and generously shared food among themselves and with friends, visitors, a passing fairy, even with Beth, the observer ("Here's a pizza I made for you").

Besides the importance of well-cooked, plentiful food, order and routine were important attributes of home. There's a time and place for everything: naps, snacks, dinners, church and school. Schedules were rigidly adhered to ("It's time for. . . ."). Regular family rituals, like birthdays, were remembered and celebrated. The houses were well organized, maintained, swept and vacuumed.

The common element in issues of order, schedules, traditions, and rituals is predictability. For children (and adults as well), knowing there is a degree of predictability in their lives—that some events will recur and some forms be maintained—is reassuring. In a fast-moving, often unstable society, predictability represents stability and ongoingness as opposed to surprise, change, and upheaval.

FAMILY RELATIONSHIPS

The function of families is to provide loving care and safe havens. The proper roles and responsibilities of individual members were generally agreed to among the children, although they sometimes needed to be reinforced or made explicit during play.

Overheard around the tree: "I have an announcement to make." Standing on the tree, "Who wants to be the father?"

Overheard in the continuing game of "family": "I want to be three years old." "No, you are ten." "But I want to be three."

Name   Date

This is my family

This is my family

Kindergartner's drawing of his family.

Family roles were played: "She's a baby girl." "She's your sister. Don't you love her?" "Bill's my grandson."

Last week's large family in the car was following in a line behind the "mother" this week. "She's our horsey," they said.

And when someone complained about a bossy mother, another child said, "Mothers are supposed to be bossy. That's their job."

For some children lumps of snow became babies to cuddle or eggs to carry.

Some of the round rocks have become eggs which are carefully hidden in the grass. "Keep this baby egg in here. We need to put it in a safe place." On another day, a child said, "The egg is comfortable with grass. I'm the doctor and came with medicine."

"Grandpa! Grandpa! Come quickly! The baby needs you!"

Being a crying baby is very popular among some. Mothers and fathers tend to rotate roles.

Family roles often included—besides the basic group of mother, father, sister, brother, and baby—grandparents, grandchildren, and sometimes uncles, aunts, and cousins. Roles were negotiated and rotated. Mothers were the basic organizers, responsible and bossy ("That's their job").

The distinction between babies and eggs was sometimes blurred. Where both existed, though, there was usually some logic in the relationship—eggs turn into babies. Also both eggs and babies are helpless, needing to be cared for and protected. Babies, a popular choice in role-playing, can be appealing and lovable or annoying and demanding—or both. The dramatic renderings of baby behavior possibly reflected the ambivalent attitudes of older siblings toward newer arrivals in their families. Love—the glue of family life—was assumed as a societal norm ("She's your sister; don't you love her?"). It was often expressed in terms of responsibility and caretaking ("We need to put it in a safe place." "She's only three weeks old—it's nap time." "We'd better take care of my sister."). Older children, particularly girls, practiced motherly roles and often had responsibility for the routines and safety of their younger siblings.

FAMILY TENSIONS

Some family scenes and relationships acted out on the playground could be upsetting to the observing adults: the conflicts, fears, and painful losses in children's out-of-school lives are suddenly and dismayingly revealed. Knowing the limitations of how the school can be of help sometimes makes it hard to watch.

One group of six children who often play family games has a meeting where roles are assigned. A child explains: "I came here to tell you that Mr. Henry had a car accident. He was driving a tow truck to bring some pigs to the farm and a car ran into the tractor." The mother begins to cry, and the children take her away, saying to me, "Can you watch this house while we go to the psychologist?" The next day they are in the same roles. "Don't you remember Mr. Henry got hit by a car? You think he died, but he is in the hospital."

"Daddy, come back home," calls the mother. The father comes. The babies lean against the wall and the father says, "I'm giving you a bobsbobs [bottle] to go to sleep." The mother leaves; the children say, "She didn't care about us." Later they come running: "Mama is turned into an old lady." And there she is—hunched over with her face distorted, lost in a scene far from us adults.

In another family game, a child said "It's lunch time. Call me 'Mom.' You never got much of a chance to see your actual mom."

And in the lilac bushes families struggle with domestic problems: "He's the father and he's mean to me but he gives the children TV's [*sic*] and games."

Overheard in a family game: "People think I'm bad because I have bad people in my family, but I'm really very good."

Not all of the enacted family dramas, of course, came from the children's direct experiences. Some were inspired by overheard family stories and some by more remote sources, particularly the media and video games. Car crashes (along with other kinds of crashes—ice bergs, space shuttles, ships) are appealing themes to children in their dramatic play. The word itself, *crash*, is expressive. When loud and drawn out ("crr—aaa—sssh!") it sounds like the actual event. Crashes have long been a staple of video games and, years before that technology was developed, "bumper cars" designed to crash into each other were commonplace in amusement parks. The children may have heard about, witnessed, or even been in real car crashes. "Driving a tow truck" to carry pigs is more in the realm of invention, a synthesis of information from several sources. Many varieties of family catastrophe provided material for dramatic action: a trip to the hospital, psychologist, or doctor. Again, some of these would have been within the immediate experience of the children, some the result of hearsay or fiction.

Relationships also provide the stuff of drama. Families don't always stay together; one or other parent, possibly both, may come and go or be permanently absent. Absences are significant elements in family dramas: the house to be cared for by a stranger when the mother is taken off; the daddy comes back but the mother leaves; a mother has been long absent, virtually unknown. Finally, the sad statement of a child, distancing himself from the "bad" members of his family, not wanting to be identified with them, represents an absence of another sort.

There is often an element of mystery in children's play—either intentional mystery or what appears mysterious because adults can't follow the train of thought or the plot. Who, in the above quote, is "Mr. Henry" and why would we think "he died"? Why and how is "mama turned into an old lady"? At times it is as though we came in halfway through the movie. We can usually pick up on the feelings behind the words, but inquiry about facts would be interruptive, invasive, and likely inhibiting. We're left guessing.

The sources of dramatic play can be equally mysterious. Ideas and impressions from multiple sources seep into the children's heads, where they are absorbed, interpreted, and transformed in play. Sharing the onus of particularly painful or frightening feelings by acting them out can relieve some of the associated stress.

ANIMAL FAMILIES

Children like to play with animals, with kittens and puppies, but they also like to be animals. Even though—or perhaps because—animal families on the playground bear a close resemblance in their habits to human families, they are popular subjects for make-believe. Possibly being an animal allows children to take a safer, more distanced view of family roles and relationships: Baby bunnies can safely rebel against parent bunnies.

In addition, transforming oneself into an animal of choice, particularly a warm-blooded animal, has lots of interesting possibilities for the imagination. Animals are similar to but different from people, and, even though the similarities are usually more evident in play, the differences allow the possibility of novelty. A cat can, for instance, turn into a gargoyle:

> Two children sit motionless on the wall posts: "I'm a cat that turns into a gargoyle."

> A "rabbit family" made a house in the corner of the wall and the school. "I love butter," said one of the bunnies. "We'll sneak down and get some while she's cooking dinner." The rabbit children came back with buttercups. "Here's sweet butter." Mother Rabbit looked

Eight-year-olds howling like wolves.

up from the fire [rocks] where she was stirring some leaves. "Honey," she said, "I told you not to do it. You're not getting roast leaves."

Family games with animals and humans flourished. A wolf family made a home with rocks and logs: "We've got tons of matching plates," said a child as she arranged some pieces of tarmac in rows near the smaller hole filled with logs. "We just eat. We don't need plates," said a child as she sat near the "bonfire."

"I am a baby squirrel."

The children play Cops and Robber and then become animals: "We're baby lions." "I'm the mother lion." "I want to be young, too." "I'm one month."

Animal games have involved many children: "This is a doggie and I'm the mother." "I'm a tiger." "I'm a cat."

Overheard at the tree, which has been home to human families and bird families: "I'm a bald eagle. I'm not born. I'm cracking my egg." And "I'm a peregrine falcon. My mom laid her egg in the air and one fell into your nest."

A unicorn, Pegasus, and a baby dragon ran around making magic. "I'm only a little dragon with fire in my tail and I haven't grown wings yet."

"We are penguins on the ice . . ."

"I'm a river otter," said Sophie sliding head first over and over again. Up by the lilac trees there is a large area of rough, thick ice where "wolves are ice skating."

Through magical transformations, children can at will become various kinds of animals and birds. These transformations are achieved through words rather than appearances or behavior: Since there were no costumes or props, the children had to explain what they were being ("I am a baby squirrel"). Age identification seemed to be an important element in the self-description and at times a matter of disagreement ("I want to be young, too"). It is not always clear if the animal itself had the right to decide his or her own age or if this was the prerogative of those organizing the play.

Although fashions change, there are some animals that are particularly popular—wolves, foxes, dogs, horses, rabbits, and various kinds of felines (cats, lions, tigers). All these are soft to the touch; most have fur, which may have something to do with their appeal—children have cuddly toy bunnies, horsies, pussies, puppies, even cuddly tigers and lions. More surprising are decisions to be an eagle or a gargoyle. But animals have qualities other than tactile that have something to do with their popularity.

The fabled characteristics associated with nondomestic, wild animals come primarily from fiction: lions are brave, horses swift, tigers and wolves are scary, eagles and falcons soar, rabbits are timid. Children act out these attributes either consistently, inconsistently, or not at all as they become the animals: Not all lions roar, not all wolves are bad.

Often the children also had some "scientific" knowledge of wild animals—one class in the school, for instance, made a study of wolves; they sometimes watched nature programs on TV or read nonfiction accounts of wild animals. There's evident "book learning" behind statements like "I'm a bald eagle. I'm not born. I'm cracking my egg"—but fantasy in the response by the peregrine falcon: "My mom laid her egg in the air and one fell into your nest." Conceptual inconsistencies can bother adults but usually not children, particularly the younger ones.

One of the remarkable features of imaginative play is how easily facts coexist with magical or mythic thinking. There's no question of reconciliation because no contradiction is seen. Stories were acted out with a cheerful combination of anthropomorphized, storybook characterizations and fairly realistic ones—different kinds of understanding seamlessly patched together.

Finally, it's tempting to wonder why children so often choose to "be" animals. What is the appeal (beyond that of taking on wonderful, mythic abilities), particularly since most of the animal families played by the children were barely distinguishable from human families? They spent a good deal of time cooking and keeping house; roles were duplicated— often that of the bossy mother and children ("Honey," she said, "I told you not to do it. You're not getting roast leaves.").

Nonetheless, there are significant differences between the lives of humans and the lives of animals that appeal to children. With some reason, they see animals' lives as free from the constraints of civilization ("We just eat. We don't need plates."). Animals don't have to attend school or church, wear shoes or other clothing. They can do what they feel like doing and have no responsibilities (unless you choose to be an animal mother and need to cook and discipline the young). Animals live in natural environments, which, particularly for city children, can seem exotic and wonderful. Caves, mountains, lakes, even jungles are created on the playground through imagined transformations.

As they grow older, having been given freedom and time to play, children tend to approach the common understanding of how the world works. Their intellectual growth, like their physical growth, is a continuum from the early years to young adulthood. However, when, how, and why they negotiate the differences between the real and the magical is mysterious, not always clear to adults. Most children are able to make conscious use of both realms. In the meantime, on the playground, children imagine, create, experiment, add to one anothers' experiences and understandings, try out ideas, try on roles. In addition to being fun, all this is serious, worthwhile learning.

☙ 2 ❧

Scary Stuff

Danger—the threat of physical or emotional hurt—is a constant element in children's imaginative lives and a familiar theme in play. On the playground, children enjoy creating tense, scary situations, which they then resolve, one way or another. Though the general outlines of the dramas are age-old (bad guys caught or cleverly evaded, villains outwitted or slain, good guys escaping, heroes triumphant), the particular situations, characters, and solutions are original, often ingenious.

CHASING, CATCHING, ESCAPING

The walls are used for jumping and running away from monsters. . . . The tree has secret locks on it that release power; sometimes it is a cage for wolves.

"We are locked in a cage. I'm the biggest wolf of all. That's why the cage is bent."

Around the tree and on the grass, the wolf games continue. Sometimes there is too much excitement in the chase, so they have to be stopped.

Chasing games are popular, with loud wolf cries. "Don't be frightened," a child said to me. "We are only wolves and wolves are good . . ."

Chasing games with monsters, "Doggie Men," aliens, and a princess being captured, have been vigorous. Temperature seems to affect the choice of games. A chilly wind makes running almost a necessity. Sometimes the tree is the launch pad for the attacks and sometimes it is the refuge.

After two weeks of playing on the hardtop we got the use of the grass area back again. Groups of children of all ages ran for the hole [they had been digging], the tree, the little house [old coal bunker], and the lilac trees. "Good" and "bad guys" chased each other everywhere, shouting, "The robot is trying to kill us!"

Spring is in the air. Children play tag or cops and robbers. It can be hard to recruit robbers. "I don't want to be a robber," is a frequent complaint. "Are you on the run or are you in jail?"

One group made a house in the corner for a mother bunny and her babies. A fox and, another day, a wolf came to scare them. Another family had a "fire" in their house in the lilac bushes, with a baby still inside. "We are trying to get her out," said Daryl.

Monsters were dangerous: "There's a monster. Let's sneak by him to get some food."

"We are the foxes," said Nancy. "They are the bunnies" (pointing to a group of nine children). "There are so many of them we can't eat them all at once, so we have to put them in a cage." They escaped with loud squeals.

Some children were put "in prison" in the hole. They ran out. "We are both beavers so we broke out with our teeth."

A family of foxes is captured by a poacher. The eagle warns them and helps them escape.

"He says he's a cheetah and he can swim in boiling lava. Nothing can live in boiling lava." We solved the problem by imagining special armor.

A policeman chased robbers. "Run! Get away!" The walls of the school and the doorways were safe havens.

Another group are adventurers. Standing on a tree, an 8-year-old says, "I'm a girl who likes to do dangerous stuff."

One can almost hear the excited screeching and sense the children's terror as they run from imagined dangers, which, in real life, they have rarely experienced. Terror is of course a wonderfully exciting feeling—for both children and adults. It intensifies life. The popularity of scary films, novels, TV programs, plays and stories, familiar to us all, attests to the attraction of terror. The children created situations on the playground that induced fear, sometimes to the point of hysteria. At this point, an adult is often needed to step in and bring the level of emotion down "before someone gets hurt" (the familiar warning).

The children drew these elements of high drama from a variety of sources—TV, literature, newspapers, hearsay (the "lore of school children"). Monsters, aliens, and robots have their roots in sci-fi; wolves, foxes, eagles are staples of myth and fable; captured princesses exist in fairy tales; cops, robbers, "good guys" and "bad guys," and jail are time-tested elements in traditional children's games; the cheetah and beavers may come from nature films or the school curriculum. The "poacher" almost undoubtedly comes from literature. In fact, it may be that children often opted for unfamiliar and unexperienced dangers because they allowed more scope for the imagination—the mystery of the unknown. The unknown can be scarier than the known—its possibilities for surprise and horror, unlimited. The terror, for instance, evoked by the shark in *Jaws* (both book and film) can be attributed in part to the mystery of "the deep," where the environment is essentially unknowable, where unseen, scary creatures lurk.

The children did not discriminate or classify; they tapped all sources available to them for their imagery, and there is no doubt of the situation's momentary credibility for them. While playing, for example, the children managed to believe that the wolves were an immediate and real threat to their lives or to the lives of other potential victims, like bunnies. They willingly consented to what they essentially knew was fictive and temporary, perhaps because they also knew they could equally well create refuges and stage escapes.

Feeling safe is the flip-side of fear. In the schoolyard, specific locations were designated as zones of safety—sometimes the walls and doorways of the school, sometimes the tree. The children could indulge in their induced feelings of fear, give them free rein, because they had built-in possibilities for relief—safe places in which they could pause, have time out so fear didn't overwhelm and exhaust them. The magical protective function of safe havens was respected through general consensus: Everyone understood and agreed to their sanctity.

Moments of doubt, though, did sometimes occur, most often when the situation was new, the plot unfamiliar with no standard "happy ending" in sight. "Nothing can live in boiling lava" is a down-to-earth, factual kind of comment. In this instance, the conflict between the believer's confidence in the cheetah's remarkable ability and nonbeliever's skepticism was solved in a satisfactory manner, with Beth's help, by resorting to magical thinking—the invention of special protective armor.

The doubter, according to Beth, knew a lot about volcanoes: "What was so fascinating was his willingness to accept the magic of armor." Expressions of skepticism, however, were relatively rare, consent more the rule.

In spite of the generally accepted dichotomy of "good" and "bad" human and animal characters, there was a surprising degree of fluidity and even ambiguity in their roles. Foxes are usually bad, but not always; the family of foxes captured by a poacher is good and is helped to escape by an eagle, though eagles are also usually bad. Wolves, ordinarily, are particularly scary, sinister, and dangerous, evoking feelings vividly expressed by a child whom I [Brenda] once heard about: being put to bed by his grandfather, he gazed nervously at the window, mumbling to himself, "It's dark as a wolf outside!"

But even wolves can be good: "Don't be frightened. We are only wolves and wolves are good." One class had made a study of wolves and, as Beth wrote, "Many of the children had learned that wolves were not the beasts they were in fairy stories."

The children, often reluctant to take on the roles of "bad" characters, were more willing when the character was particularly impressive or powerful: "I'm the biggest wolf of all." But there were always some who shrank from scary play altogether. Unable or unwilling, for their own reasons, to deal with fear in this way, they might have gone off alone or taken up a different group activity. Up to a point, though, for most children, acting out terrors in a safe schoolyard context, in addition to being fun, can be reassuring. An imaginary wolf lurking outside the bedroom door or even hiding under the bed at night is terrifying; in the light of day, a similar wolf, though still scary, can be controlled or outwitted, allowing the child the upper hand and a comforting sense of power. Also, feelings of terror, when intentionally evoked on the playground, have understood limits: The game can always be called off, the wolf banished into thin air. The escape valve for the traditional childhood compact, "let's pretend," is a return to everyday reality.

CATASTROPHES

The tree became a spaceship: "It's going up—the space shuttle." "I'm the shuffle man. One, two, three . . ." "The spaceship blowed up."

The wall and lilac trees became the Titanic: "Get on that tree 'cause there's an iceberg coming!"

One day the walls became motorcycles and spaceships, while
the steps became a car for a large family of 5-to-7-year-olds who
were dealing with a medical emergency. There were five babies,
a mother, a father, a big sister, and a friend. "We're going to the
hospital," said a child. "Barb broke her head open. She got crashed
from a car." "Who knows how to drive?" asked the father. "Big
Sister, drive the car," ordered the mother.

"We're playing princess and bad guys; I'm the bad guy and she's
about to execute me."

"I'm the captain of the pirate ship." "The boat is blowing," said Kali.
"It's going to blow everything and the people will die."

Some of the catastrophes acted out by the children were based on
horrific real events, once reported in the newspapers and subsequently
mythologized through retellings and reenactments over time.

The blowing up of the space shuttle *Challenger* happened in 1986,
within the recent memory of the parents and grandparents of the schoolchildren. The tragedy was given extra poignancy and immediacy by the
death of the on-board schoolteacher, Christa McAuliffe, one of the first
women to venture into space. The children at the Mission Hill School had
undoubtedly heard the story, perhaps even read about it in school books.

Though the sinking of the luxury liner *Titanic*, on its maiden voyage,
dates back to 1912, before the First World War, it has always held a place
in the popular imagination—a huge tragedy in which more than half of
the 1,500 passengers died. The discovery of the hull at the bottom of the
ocean in 1985 and the romantic 1997 movie starring Kate Winslet and
Leonardo DiCaprio revived general interest in the catastrophe. The children's knowledge of the *Titanic* probably came directly or indirectly from
the film, though their focus was more on the image of the iceberg and
the frightening crash than the movie-version romantic tale. Beth recol-
lects that "they played the *Titanic* over and over." Who knows how they
pictured the threat of the iceberg "coming"?

Both these disasters, the sinking of the *Titanic* and the explosion of
the space shuttle, were national traumas as well as subjects of ongoing,
intense national interest. Both events were retold and reenacted many
times over, in film, books, and the media—ways, perhaps, in which adults
attempted to deal with the shock and horror of what had happened (as
well as, more cynically, the media's usual opportunism in encouraging
sales and reaching wider audiences). Children, picking up on the associated feelings of sadness and fear, created their own versions of these, to
them, essentially abstract events. Strong feelings provided the energy for

high-action drama and, as for adults, a way of repeating and thus taking the edge off their intensity.

In my [Brenda's] own childhood, back in the third decade of the last century, the Lindbergh case was the national trauma: Charles and Anne Lindbergh's infant son was kidnapped from his crib, the body found much later by the side of a road. The kidnapper had evidently propped a ladder against the side of the house in order to gain entry to the baby's nursery on the second floor. The event itself, then its aftermath—including a ransom note, payment, and the trial of the apprehended kidnapper—were in the newspapers daily. The Lindbergh drama was the daily subject of dinner table conversation among our parents and their friends. My older sister, friends, and I reenacted the kidnapping for months, taking turns being the baby, borrowing a ladder as prop. Our fascination with the case stemmed from its prominence in the news and the anxious conversation of our elders, intensified by our fear for ourselves. According to my dim memory of that time, we were concerned for our own safety, felt personally threatened. My sister remembers looking out of her bedroom window nightly before going to bed, to make sure a ladder was not propped against the wall. Reenacting the kidnapping was a way of reducing fear and a kind of exorcism against potential evil energized by the attraction of spine-tingling drama. We enjoyed it for months.

Family emergencies—injuries, accidents, hospitals—were common experiences in the lives of Mission Hill School children. Their knowledge here was firsthand, real and convincing. In fact, perhaps because of its familiarity, "the trip to the hospital" may have been less terrifying, more ordinary, than icebergs or exploding shuttles, more what life is like. Even Barb's head injury seems to have been dealt with rather matter-of-factly. Acting out and objectifying family tensions and crises may in fact make them appear less traumatic, more simply a matter of how things are.

In the invented setting—with princesses and bad guys—it is startling to hear one of the latter announce that he is to be "executed." The word itself, *executed*, is sophisticated. One wonders where it came from. We will never know whether the sentence was carried out or if the speaker was rescued at the last minute. I tend to think the latter. Finally, Kali's pirate ship seems to derive characteristics from both the *Titanic* and the space shuttle; it is "going to blow everything and the people will die."

DEATH

Children dug for worms. There were arguments about what to do with them. Some children wanted to feed a worm to the turtle.

Others objected passionately. "No, Poor little worm. You don't know what it feels like to die." "I don't care," said the other child. But he put the worm down.

Another day several worms were found and again the argument came up: "You don't know what it feels like to die. Let it go." "I'd be feeling I'm dead." "Would you feel bad? Put it back and cover it up."

Dandelions were made into necklaces and gathered in bunches and put on a bird's grave: "We have a dead bird. We need your [Beth's] help to bury it."

"Remember when we buried a blue jay last year and people kept digging it up? It's now dirt and rock." And the next day: "Joe wants to see it," so children dug up the bird and reburied it.

"We are burying the fairy," said Jamie and Jade. "The fairy died. One of the trolls got him."

Two older girls, watched by younger children, were huddled in the grass over a computer diskette. "Disky died and we had a funeral. Now we're performing an autopsy, and then we're going to put it back together again." "That's gauze and that holds the information." Later: "We were successful in putting it together and now we are burying it. We'll all rise and sing the disk's favorite song: Yankee Doodle." After the burial, the girl wrote this on a stone: "Born September 12, 1998; Died June 2, 1999. R.I.P."

Death continues to fascinate the children. One day a group rolled large leaves into cigar shapes and carried them to the "pyramid" where the salamander mummy is buried. "We found three dead animals—a bee, a moth, and a worm. We are burying them in the pyramid."

And one hot day, a six-year-old walked around with a small notebook and pen. She went from shady place to shady place, sitting on a wall, a log, a tree. At the end of playtime, she said to me, "You know why I want to write by myself? Someone died and I want to write. It sort of makes me feel better." Then she read to me what she had written: "Time will pass / But I will never forget you. / Time will pass / But I will never forget you."

Children at Mission Hill School, like children everywhere, were deeply concerned with death, with trying to take in the meaning of permanent, irreversible loss. They were also concerned with what death is like for the person who is dying and what it "feels like" to be buried. The mystery surrounding the near-forbidden subject is intensified by the general discomfort of adults in discussing it. Parents and caretakers are understandingly evasive, often unwilling to confront children with the bleak, tragic, inevitable, and painful facts of death in the face of which they are helpless. It is hard to respond in comforting ways to children's age-old pleas like, "Tell me you'll never leave me; tell me I'm never going to die."

There is, of course, the comfort and reassurance of religion. On the playground the children made frequent use of religious emblems and rituals. They showed themselves to be familiar with the ceremonies around death—mourning, wakes, funerals, burials—which they simulated, using whatever came to hand or mind: flowers on the grave, music ("We'll all rise and sing the disk's favorite song: Yankee Doodle"), inscription on the gravestone, even burial practices revived from ancient Egypt (procession to the pyramid to bury the dead salamander).

Established rituals link a particular death to those which have come before and to those which will come after, providing some consolation in this way for those bereft. Although for the children, the subject of mourning could be almost anyone or anything (from a fairy to a diskette), it might be said that they are practicing dealing with the feelings and circumstances of death. The company of others during ceremonies and mourning lessens its scariness.

As they enacted scenes of death, the children were, incidentally, exercising some of the school's pedagogical principles, or habits of mind: for instance, viewpoint, "stepping into the shoes of . . ."—in this case, a dead worm—and relevance, the personal meaning of loss. (For discussion of habits of mind, see Chapter 5.)

In spite of their sorrow and professed empathy for dead creatures, the children also showed themselves to be hard-headed and realistic. Asked how he would feel if he were dead, a child responded, "I'd be feeling I'm dead." Another commented, "When I was little I tasted dirt and it didn't taste bad." They were intrigued by the science of decomposition ("Now it's dirt and rock") and were curious enough to dig up and rebury dead creatures.

The imaginative play around the theme of death is reminiscent of the classic wartime French film *Forbidden Games*. In it, a little girl's parents and her dog are killed by Nazi planes strafing a stream of escaping refugees. The child is taken in by a French peasant family whose 10-year-old son becomes her friend. The two children create together a secret cemetery in which they first bury her dog, then a series of other dead animals from the neighborhood. They steal crosses from a nearby cemetery to mark the graves. The film implies that the child is ritualizing her overwhelming feelings of loss, playing "forbidden games" as a way of dealing with her own close, traumatic, and premature experience of death.

The arts, of course, are akin to play in their use of imagination and invention. The child who secluded herself to write a poem has chosen another form in which to express and thus assuage her grief: "It sort of makes me feel better."

❧ 3 ☙

The Environment

HOLES AND ROCKS

Within the first few weeks of school, in the fall of 1998, the children began to dig. They dug with sticks and their feet. They found an old spoon in the tall grass by the fence and dug with that. In October the school bought some trowels, shovels, hoes, and rakes so the children could plant bulbs in the front of the school. The children asked to use the tools at play time, and with my [Beth's] help, they set aside a space near the chain-link fence for digging. During the last days of October and all of November some children dug each play time. Some of the holes became large enough to collect standing water during rains. Children jumped over them.

In the first week in December, two 9-year-old boys asked for shovels so they could dig in one of the holes near the fence. They were joined by other children who took turns digging; by the end of play time, the hole was big enough to stand in. The next group of children to come out saw the hole and filled it with leaves and jumped over and in it. During the next week, the children dug two other large holes and several smaller ones. The turf was dug up carefully and arranged in a circle to make a "fairy garden." Some 30 children, ages 5 to 10, worked in groups to dig the holes. Their purposes? "To reach China." "To get worms for Yertle and Myrtle [classroom turtles]. They eat two worms a day." "To find artifacts and bones."

> Some of the round rocks which were dug up became "eggs" which were carefully hidden in the grass.

> In another week the two larger holes had become one very large hole and the children dug frantically.

> Three children watched as the diggers dug up a stone. A boy shouted, "Take it away, people. We need to work here." "Isn't it pretty?" said a child as she took the stone. "It's gold."

Children "inspecting" the hole.

Winter 1998–1999: In the last schoolweek in December, the diggers struck a large stone. Children dug around it and finally one of the older girls, Alice, and I [Beth] rolled it up the side of the hole.

> "It weighs about the same as James," said a child. "James, how much do you weigh?" "Fifty pounds," he answered. Three nine-year-old children stood in the hole. They then tried to lift the stone. "Roll it," said Kyle.

> They rolled it to the fairy garden where they made a semi-circular wall around the space, using all the rocks they could find. One child said it was a piece of quartz. [In the first few weeks of school, some classes had identified minerals as they studied the neighborhood.]

> The effort to get the stone out involved 30 or more children at different times. Five-year-olds did their part and learned to push the shovel into the ground. After it was out, a group of 5- and 6-year-olds began to use some of the displaced earth to make a mound.

"We are burying the fairy," said Jamie and Jade. "The fairy died. One of the trolls got him."

In January, the children came back from vacation to find that the hole was covered in ice. They slid on it and tried to batter it with logs. As the ice broke, they picked up the pieces and pretended the bits of ice were babies and animals. When the ice melted and the bottom of the hole became mud, children with boots squished in it, while those without boots looked on from the sides.

"I love the mud," said a child as she slid in the mud. "It's the greatest thing. You get dirty."

Ice prevents access to the grass area. Several children said, "I would like to go see what has happened in the hole." Perhaps someone will be able to crawl up to give a report.

In February, they were able to go back onto the grassy area, and they rushed to the hole and found it had changed. There were rocks in the bottom, and the sides were not so steep. "Someone filled it up," said one child when she saw rocks frozen in the bottom. Had the rain changed it? They covered it with logs; when the logs fell in and the temperature dropped and the logs froze, they worked to get them out. Three younger children took the logs and put them in a small hole.

"We're pretending it's a fire and she is standing in it." Sheila went to a smaller hole and lay in it and said, "I'm pretending I'm a baby sleeping."

Sliding on the ice in the hole and battering free the logs from the ice continued to involve boys and girls of all ages. They argued as they crushed the ice: "We started the hole." "No. We did." In the end I recalled that both groups started holes and the two holes grew into one. Pieces of ice were taken out of the hole as soon as they were freed and became valuable for children to hoard and hold.

On Tuesday children tried to dig in the holes but could only scoop a little dirt from the top layer. "It is still frozen." So for a few days there was no more digging.

Some days the hole was a swimming pool. One day the large hole became a cage for bunnies.

Spring 1999: The hole continued to fascinate some children. Two girls (who said their mothers did not mind their getting muddy) dug with sticks in the hole.

> By April, the hole was much deeper, but the goal was no longer China. "We want to reach water," said the diggers.

> The hole gets deeper. "We are digging to water." "That's not good. The school will get flooded."

By May, a large piece of stone had begun to emerge. A teacher said she thought it might be a conglomerate of cement and stone; a child said, "But that is what a pudding stone is—only it is thousands of years old." In the fall, when the school studied the neighborhood, some children had gone up the street to an old quarry of Roxbury pudding stone.

By the end of May, the pudding stone was free and the children tried to get it out of the hole. Seven 7-year-olds asked an 11-year-old to help them lift one end of the stone while they put a log under it. They continued to lift and add a log.

> "We used the logs to move it. We pushed it up a bit. We put logs under it and we rolled it up. We made a track out of logs across the grass to the wall."

It was a lot bigger than the 44-pound chunk of quartz they had dug up earlier in the winter. A visitor carried it into the school, and it was found to weigh 70 pounds. The digging continued; the hole was now 3 to 4 feet deep by 2 yards across and became the setting for various make-believe games.

> "Excuse me sir, I think I sprained my ankle. Have pity please," said a child as she fell into the hole where a boy was standing.

> "We are playing avalanche. Everyone has to get in the middle and then we push the dirt and rocks."

> After the rain there was water in the hole, and snails, and footprints. "I think it's a raccoon," said Katie. Later she said, "It's a clue that it's a raccoon. We found some grubs and I think raccoons eat grubs."

Fall 1999: In September of the next schoolyear, children went back to digging in the hole.

"Can you believe this hole stayed here all summer?"

"It's like making the pyramids."

One day the hole was filled with logs. There was an argument over which group of children could play in the hole. "This is our archaeological site." "No it is our rabbit stew. It has been cooking for a week. It'll be ready soon, tomorrow maybe."

When the hole became packed hard from children running and jumping in it, a plank was put across and the children walked across carefully because there were "monsters" below. One day they played Billy Goats Gruff. Various kinds of bridges were built over the hole and the strength of each was tested. "The bridge is wobbly and I might fall in." "We like it wobbly. It is more challenging. There are alligators there."

Winter 1999–2000: After the balmy weather came the cold. "There is ice in the postholes," said Keisha. Later, as she stirred, she said, "It's almost melting—and dirt will make it mud." The children played around and in the hole and dug in it during this second winter.

Spring 2000: In March the hole was larger.

"Look I can run around it like a race track," said a seven-year-old boy who then stood in it and stroked the sides.

When it was filled with melting snow some children put logs in it and laid a plank over the logs, "We are going down the river."

In April, the hole was filled with rainwater; the children measured the depth by making marks on the sides.

Children walk on floating logs across it. "I can do it with my eyes shut," says a child in boots.

When the water retreated, 15 children took turns digging until, by the end of April, the hole was wide and deep enough for 6 or 7 children to stand in together.

"The water level was up to here," said a boy, pointing to the top line on the side of the hole.

Lukas (staff member) needed some dirt so three children filled boxes for him, conversing as they dug: "We need a world dictionary. We need to find out all about things. This is dirt. It's part earth, rocks, and dead things." "I found a crystal rock. Maybe it's a baby of the big one we took inside last year."

Older children at the second play time took all the rocks and logs out of the hole and began to dig the hole deeper. A group of younger children put a plank against the wall and carried mud from the hole to cover the plank. Why?

It's amazing to see how the children respect the area of another person's dig. There have been a few complaints that someone "took my shovel when I just put it down" or "She lifted it too high and hit me with dirt." But by the following week children were sharing tools and working together. Even the usual "bosses" of the dig have given their tools to younger children and helped them to dig "the right way." When it is time to put the tools away, the children bring them down without having to be asked more than once.

Children make connections to what they have been studying. "Come look we're digging a special rock," shouts Kali. Five children dig with sticks near the walkway. "We are finding treasure." "We're going to find a rock from a long time ago." Jessica hears this exchange and runs over. She helps unearth a piece of clinker. "Look, we found a meteorite," she says. More pieces are unearthed so that each child has a piece. They show the pieces to Joyce [staff member] who brings in a piece of coal for them to compare. Some of the children go down into the basement of the school to see the old coal burning furnace and talk about coal burning and the clinker that is left.

Children collected rocks. "I wrote 50 on the rock because it is so big," said a 5-year-old. "It must be 50 years old."

Days of rain fill the hole with water. Children float logs in it and jump over it. "Let's look for ancient history," said Tenisha as she poked a stick in the mud.

Digging continued the following year, but no new large stone was found.

Why is digging so universally fascinating and why do children put such strenuous, determined efforts into it even when "nothing is found"? There is, of course, always the hope—usually, for children, the expectation—that something remarkable will be found. Through their active imaginations, the children digging in the playground usually made their wishes come true. They turned common, everyday stones into exciting, wonderful finds ("It's gold." "We're finding treasure.").

Beyond the excitement of these anticipated finds there was the added drama of excavation itself: The ordinary rocks they dug up, both small and large, had been concealed for unimaginable lengths of time in the dark, mysterious ground until on a particular day and hour they were literally unearthed by the children, revealed to the light.

There are, however, two further basic motivations for young children to dig, both antecedent to expectation and drama: First, they dig because they can, because the ground is diggable, almost invites digging. Young children want to do whatever appears possible as they explore and test the physical world. An infant drops a spoon, watching it fall to the floor (after the adult has returned it, perhaps two dozen times, to the high-chair tray); a toddler pulls a wooden donkey with wheels on a cord and turns to see it miraculously following her; a 2-year-old slaps a sink full of water, splashing it with delight on the wall and floor. And where there's ground, children want to dig.

Then there is wonder, one of the defining characteristics of childhood. The children undoubtedly wondered about what might be down there and whether they could find out and even whether they would be allowed to investigate. As they began to dig, they wondered about the mysterious, the unseen and unknown, about the fabled (reaching China) and half-understood (finding water).

Edith Cobb (1977), in *The Ecology of Imagination in Childhood*, describes this quality of mind: "Wonder is itself a kind of expectancy of fulfillment. The child's sense of wonder, displayed as surprise and joy, is aroused as a response to the mystery of some external stimulus that promises 'more to come' or better still 'more to do'—the power of perceptual participation in the known and unknown" (p. 2).

The unknown became the known, or at least the seen, when the rocks had been dug out. The larger ones required time, hard work, and group effort to dig around and eventually leverage up out of the hole and move onto level ground, where they could be examined. Then came further observations and speculation ("Maybe it's the baby of the big one we took inside last year"), assessment ("It weighs about the same as James"), and identification ("It's a giant piece of puddingstone"). The children, like adult scientists, shared perceptions and information—that pudding stone, for instance, is "a conglomerate many thousands of years old." Some statements, to be sure, were questionable, such as the confident conclusion of a 5-year-old that "it is so big; it must be 50 years old" or the discovery of a "meteorite." Some shared information they had learned in school about the formation and age of pudding stone and the composition of dirt.

Aside from the material dug out, the holes themselves were of great interest to the children. These changed in response to the seasons of the schoolyear and their own efforts. By late spring of the first year, the hole was impressive: "3 or 4 feet deep and 2 yards wide." In the fall, it filled with water, which froze during the winter months. The surrounding ground became hard, and all digging had to be suspended. At one point, when ice prevented the children from visiting the hole, they wondered what had "happened." Changes in the shape, contents, and texture of the holes were noted and wondered at: "Someone filled it up." "The sides aren't as steep." Beth commented that "The rain had changed the hole," followed by a question, "or was it the after-school kids?" In the spring, digging resumed and the hole became even deeper. That fall, at the opening of school, a child was surprised and probably pleased that it had "stayed here all summer." All these observed transformations were exciting—dirt to mud to water to ice and back to mud; soft to hard to soft, shallow to deep and wide.

In the course of the excavation and its aftermath, the children experienced basic physical phenomena like leverage, resistance, inertia, gravity, and balance. They learned, through their bodies, how these dynamics work in practical situations—leveraging up a heavy rock and wedging logs under it to maintain its position; the comparative ease of rolling rather than dragging a rock; and, of course, the weight itself of the rocks and dirt, which "resist" being removed, and the tendency of everything to slide back into the hole. Later, studying physics in school, they may encounter and, because of their work on the playground, more deeply understand the meaning of terms like *fulcrum* and *mechanical advantage*.

A considerable amount of social learning also took place around the hole. The task itself of removing such large quantities of heavy stone and earth required the collaboration, at times, of up to 30 children. No teachers directed the operation, and, in spite of occasional disputes over ownership and about the use of implements ("She hit me with dirt"), it was successful. In time, the holes got dug, one of them of impressive size. The older children, "the bosses," took turns with the younger ones using the shovels and instructing them in the correct use of tools. The children's intense common interest in the success of the cooperative endeavor, driven by the mystery and excitement of discovery, kept them at it, kept children of different ages working together.

Semiscientific interest in the nature of the excavation did not close out imaginative play and fantasy. As usual on the playground, fact and fancy were virtually inseparable, the former leading to the latter through the power of suggestion: A mound formed by some of the displaced earth suggested a burial mound for fairies; logs, even frozen ones, suggested fire. When the ground was too hard for digging, the children invented uses for the hole—a bonfire, swimming pool, and café for bunnies. Some play was reality-based even if the events being acted out were highly unlikely. Unlike fairies, avalanches actually do exist. So do snakes. And reaching water is a likely outcome of persistent digging.

The children had strong feelings of ownership about the hole—their own creation, which they knew well and had observed through many changes. Their sense of responsibility and familiarity bordered at times on an odd kind of affection: "A seven-year-old boy spends his playtime gently stroking and marking the side of the hole as he stands in it."

Most encouraging perhaps in terms of education in general was the deep engagement of the children in the excavations and their appetite for further learning: "We need a world dictionary. We need to find out all about things." "Let's look for ancient history." "We are going to find a rock from a long time ago."

Most adults, even in urban settings, have childhood memories that share the basic qualities of the playground experiences described above— exploring, shaping, and transforming nature. Many adults remember digging "to China," floating twigs in the gutter, breaking up ice in a puddle, making tunnels in sand—all those invented and reinvented activities. And they remember how much fun they were. Such adventures almost always took place not in, but out of school and away from adults. Even now, as we recognize the educational value of free exploration of the natural world, it is not given time or space in school, even in kindergarten.

Two enabling conditions pertained at the Mission Hill School that made the children's diggings possible. First was the unstructured, rather messy status of the outdoor area (described in the Introduction). The school was located in a former high school building. The outdoor space was run down, had not been cared for in years, and, not having been designed for young children in the first place, there were no play structures, no areas meant for particular games or activities. There were, however, bushes, an area of blacktop, grass, dirt, different levels of ground, a steep bank, and wall at the back. The children had to invent ways to play in this fenced-off space, which of course they did. Most contemporary school buildings are surrounded by hardtop with areas beneath the play equipment covered with cork, wood chips, or composite materials. Planted areas are off-limits to play. It's hard to know how to intentionally design open-ended, "messy" space. But, if the value of such space is clear and recognized, then some of its positive qualities can be built into the design of playgrounds.

The second condition was the level of risk the digging involved—children wielding shovels, balancing themselves on planks over the deep hole, rolling heavy logs, acting on their own authority. There were always adults present, to be sure, and safety rules (e.g., no throwing of stones) were enforced. Nonetheless, the children were given lots of leeway and responsibility for their own safety with the tacit understanding that it was in their own interest not to get hurt. It's worth quoting here a sign at the entrance to the Diana, Princess of Wales, Memorial Playground in the northeast corner of Kensington Park, London:

> "The facilities provided are designed to comply with European and British legislation. However, it is now recognized that risk taking is an important element of play and physical development. Parents and carers [*sic*] must note that the design of this playground does allow for a degree of risk. This is intentionally provided so your child can develop an appreciation of risk in a controlled play environment rather than taking similar risks in the uncontrolled and unregulated wider world."

Serious injuries were in fact notably rare at Mission Hill School.

CREATURES

The foundation of natural science is observation. Observation and shared discovery were part of the daily drama on the playground.

> Children dug for worms. There were arguments about what to do with them. Some children wanted to feed a worm to the turtle. Another objected passionately.

> Gibrat let her salamander free. "I want to visit him sometimes," she said as she put him through the fence.

> "Look, there's a hawk on the fence." The children ran to see it and it flew up to perch on the drainpipe outside Geralyn's classroom. "It's heard there are mice in the room and it's come to get them." Some children thought it had a hurt leg. During the two play times, it perched in different places on the school, moving its head and looking down at the children. "See, it likes us." Children told stories of hawks near their houses and one child thought this hawk might have followed him "from my house to school."

"Woolly bear" caterpillar.

"Look—the butterfly laid eggs on the leaf."

"That's maybe an insect. It looks like a fly that's a dragon."

A group of 5- to 7-year-olds have discovered snails. Unlike the children two years ago, they handle them with gentle care and put them back in the leaves at the end of playtime. One day they lined up 15 or more snails on a log. "I'm getting a friend. Come here, little girl," said one child as she carefully placed a snail on a log. "I'm a day-care worker. I take care of snails."

"I know they lay eggs," said another as she found a baby snail. "I read that last year in a book."

The big girls came back to make a clubhouse in the lilac trees. This time the space was shared: "Look, there are snails in the tree." "That one doesn't have a shell. It will die." "No, it is a slug. They don't have shells." "Let's put them through the fence and see if they come back tomorrow."

"Look, the worm made an S," said Louis.

A bumblebee, circling around the flowers, frightened some children and delighted others: "Look at his fur."

"Come, look. I saw some animal tracks." We followed the tracks along the wall of the school to the front fence, then back along the wall to the path and the steps to the gate going to the convent. "It must have been a raccoon." "Maybe a dog." "Too small. A dog couldn't get through."

"I love snakes," said a child observing a small garter snake curled into a corner of the step. "Don't touch it. Let it be." Word spread and soon children came running over to see the snake. No one tried to pick it up or poke it with a stick as they did last year.

Another day a child came to tell me, "We found a salamander. You can't touch it 'cause the oil on your hands will kill it. It penetrates their skin." The tiny reptile was gently slipped onto a piece of cardboard while children crowded around to see it. It was then put through the fence into the long grass.

Children making fairy houses dug up a big earthworm. A new child shrieked. The child holding it said, "You want to touch it?" Very slowly the new girl did. Later, she took it to a hole she was digging, checking again still later "to see if he was safe."

"Look, I found a baby ant where I found them last year. I'll take it in to our ant farm." "Come look. See what we found under the rock."

Margo came to me one day. "They say spiders are bad. They're not." I followed her to where children were mixing mud in the post holes in the wall and we talked about spiders. It was a new idea for the children that one of them considered spiders good and could explain why she thought so.

Positive feelings about larger animals—horses, dogs, elephants, even lions and tigers—are usual for children (see the Chapter 1 section "Animal Families"). However, many children's reactions to bugs, snakes, worms, and other small creatures vary from horror (often leading to cruelty) to disgust. At Mission Hill School, children from families that had

had experiences hiking and camping—usually middle-class families—were initially more likely to feel comfortable with small living creatures on the playground. These children communicated bits of information and feelings of acceptance to the others, influencing them in positive ways (another demonstration of the advantages of diverse school populations).

In general, as the children became more familiar on the playground with the resident snakes, worms, bees, salamanders, butterflies, snails, spiders, and ants, their initial feelings of suspicion and fear moderated, often turning into curiosity, even affection, and humane concern ("I love snakes"). Many became deeply interested in the life gradually revealed in the dirt, plants, trees, and among the rocks. And often they identified with it. These small and often surprising survivors in a basically unfriendly environment became ongoing subjects of investigation and drama and were treated with tender care ("I'm a day-care worker. I take care of snails.").

Much of children's natural empathy comes from their ability to easily anthropomorphize the creatures being observed—to transfer to them their own kinds of feelings: "See, it [the hawk] likes us." They felt keenly for the worm when it was suggested as food for the classroom turtle, and they planned visits (however unlikely) to a liberated salamander. They were again practicing one of the school's recommended habits of mind: viewpoint (taking another's perspective even when the "other" was a bug or reptile).

Along with their imaginative projections, the children became natural scientists, closely observing, noticing, and discussing the characteristics of the creatures on the playground: "It looks like a fly that's a dragon."

Seven-year-old's drawing of Monarch butterfly.

A butterfly's eggs were spotted on a leaf; a child noted the S shape in the dirt, made by a worm; a group admired a bumblebee's "fur." They extended the information derived from direct observation with facts learned from the school curriculum, from books, from conversations and other untraceable sources: "I know they lay eggs. I read that last year in a book." "Don't touch it 'cause the oil on our hands will kill it. It penetrates their skin."

Exclamations of "Look!" and "Come look!" were heard frequently on the playground, particularly in the warmer months when small-scale life was more active and visible. The words heralded an exciting discovery along with the children's urgent need to share, to communicate to others, the wonder of what had been found. The excitement of the discoverers was contagious, often drawing a crowd of other children. Something of a common culture thus developed among the schoolchildren—one of intense interest in, and respect for, living things and appreciation of their special qualities. This culture, and its characteristic mingling of fancy and fact, was supported by the supervising adults and often carried over into the classrooms. Children were less likely than in the early days of the school to throw stones at snakes, "freak out" at spiders, or find worms disgusting.

WEATHER

Weather and the changing seasons had a strong influence on outdoor play. The nature of the children's activities depended on what was out there (growing things or snow and ice), what was possible (when, for instance, the temperature was below 32°F), and what mood was suggested by the quality of the particular season (the "euphoria," for instance, of spring). The cyclical disappearance and reappearance of living things from September to June stimulated the children's curiosity and imagination.

In the fall, there were still nostalgic reminders of summer warmth along with anticipations of the coming winter cold.

[The children] are still digging, rolling logs, playing on tree.

Do you wonder what we do when it rains as it did last Tuesday? The children choose one of four activity rooms [reading and quiet games, art and music, dance and gymnastics, computer and blocks].

Pointing to some clover growing from a crack in the wall, "How do they make this?" "You mean the seeds are in there?"

Seven-year-old's drawing of leaf.

Smiling children came running up to me with a dandelion. "Look. That's the only flower left." "We found it sticking through the fence." "We're going to use it for a magic potion."

Observations of nature continue. Dandelion "clocks" are blown; the flowers called "bacon-and-eggs" are still being gathered, and fungi "like yoghurt" have appeared on the bark of the tree. Two new students found snails.

A worm house is built "so the worms won't be freezing in the fall and winter."

> "It was a rainbow that I
> Saw a long, long time ago
> and I drew it so I Could
> remember it."
>   9/23/99

"A Rainbow": Story by six-year-old dictated to teacher.

When the temperature dropped, snow and ice became the most interesting features of the playground, enabling many kinds of activities and investigations.

Sliding on the ice in the hole and battering free the logs from the ice continued to involve boys and girls of all ages.

The snow banks along the wall are walked on, run on, and climbed on. As small Ethan walked along the irregular ridge, he said, "I went to the beach in Puerto Rico."

There is a tunnel, or a bridge, on the largest snow bank. It was strong enough for Carol and Nancy's father to walk across it. Several children brought their dolls to play in the snow.

It was a short week with snow the highlight of activity. The plow left great piles of it on the basketball court. Children of all ages climbed and ran on the piles, rolled down them, and chased each other everywhere. Carefully they climbed on the tree, trying to brush snow off the branches and trunk.

One 5-year-old found a way to prevent himself from throwing snowballs. He took off his gloves. Why? I asked. "So I don't throw snow," he said. "My hands will get cold if I pick it up and I will remember."

There was some snow left on the hardtop on Monday, and children discovered new things about it. "Put the mud ball right here," said one child indicating a puddle surrounded by snow. "It will look beautiful in the snow." She mixed the mud into the snow with her foot. "See, it's beautiful."

Winter

Snow flakes
fall like A so-
ft feather. Covering
the ground like A dlank-
et. All the animals go
away. Until next sprin-
g they come back to
play

"Winter": Poem by seven-year-old.

A 6-year-old paused in her flurry of activity to observe that "where there is no shade, it [the snow] is soft; where there is shade, it is hard."

In spite of its predictability, spring is always somehow a surprise, a recurrent "miracle." The return of warmth and color, the softening of outlines in nature, allow children a kind of physical freedom—from indoor constraints and the burden of heavy clothing—and the world once more seems open and benign. The children expressed spring exuberance through heightened physical activity—chasing, climbing, running, and jumping. The rushing about was complemented, however, by renewed attention to details and close observation of nature.

On the grass and around the tree there was continuous activity, chasing games, climbing, jumping, balancing on logs, digging holes, and observation of ants, fungus, and a garter snake.

One day when they couldn't agree on a game, children practiced climbing, balancing, and jumping. "This is my front row seat," said Tiffie astride a branch. "I'm going to do the moonwalk, everybody," said Arnie as he walked on another branch.

Children have pretended to be rock-climbing on the tree.

The grassy areas provide a natural laboratory for observations and tactile experiences that interest and delight children. They find snails, salamanders, garter snakes, ants, earthworms, bees, butterflies, spiders and beetles to examine. They do not kill them as they did two years ago because a large group of children now protect the animals. "Let it have a life" is a phrase we cherish.

At the tree, children examined the trunk where the bark is coming off and devised theories to explain the meaning of the designs they found on the tree's inner surface. "There were worms inside the bark and they crawled up and made designs." "They look like the brain coral reef." (The children had seen a video about coral reefs that morning.) "It's a kind of Morse Code."

Discovering the bulbs we planted in the fall are in bloom; finding buds on the lilac tree—all this happened in one week [in March].

Lilacs in bloom, picking buttercups. . . . The grass on the terraces is long and has become a jungle.

The lilac tree is beloved, and I [Beth] was greeted when I returned from my absence with, "You missed the most beautiful flowers, but they are still beautiful." Looking at the daffodils through the fence, a five-year-old said, "They're popping up."

Dandelions are in bloom. Children picked them to make necklaces, to put on top of a filled hole, to make a nest on the tree, to make "a fairy house we can carry around," to place in front of a rock and wooden "shrine," and to be carried in a tight mass: "Look what I made. I tied six together."

Bark, stones, wood, grass, and mud are important props. Lizzie held a piece of bark to her ear as she said, "The robber is down there."

A group of girls makes a "garden," planting apple and orange seeds in the grass. "Look—here are some seeds," says a child as she breaks open an apple. When I say we could get the tools and dig a garden near the wall where the seeds might have a chance to grow, they jump up and dance around.

A group of classrooms planted a gingko tree and a flowering cherry tree in front of the school. A group of sixth graders are making a raised garden in hopes of growing some Chinese vegetables.

In front of the school, the trees have to be watered and the gardens tended. One group of 6th graders is building a gazebo for the garden.

"We invented a chemical to make things grow faster—at least we're trying to," said Jai as he mixed some dirt.

House building is "the spring thing." But problems abound: How can a group of fairy houses made with small sticks and grass be preserved? "We might get a fairy watchdog to guard it."

"We make fairy houses in the spring when it's wet," a child explains. "That's when they need protection."

Fairy houses were built by different groups and with different materials. One group used bark and rocks; the other, mud and grass and buttercups and a "large leaf to be a shade stuff." They sang as they built: "Look at these buttercups. The fairies will come tonight. They like to live in it."

Six children built "contraptions" in the stumps of the privet hedge, balancing pieces of bark, sticks, and rocks in the slim branches. The wind was strong. "It's holding out against the wind," said a child.

Children, unlike most adults, tend to experience all weather as positive—unless they had been specifically cautioned against the hazards of the outdoors. Some of the Mission Hill children lived in dangerous neighborhoods and, as young children, had been kept by their parents safely indoors, not allowed to play outside their homes. When they came to the school, they seemed somewhat apprehensive outside the building. The unfamiliar experience of being in an apparently less protected, less structured, more exposed environment made them uncertain. The vagaries of the weather itself caused uneasiness. This group of children had never, in Beth's words, "been out on rough grass, faced wind, or felt rain, never played in the snow." Gradually they learned, from their own

Water

Fizzy like Soda

Chily like ice

Clear like a new window

Dirty like mice

Green like a sour apple

Brown like dirt

these are water's great forms

water is in a waterbed

water drizzles from the clouds falling falling non stop water is wet water is great fahh water

"Water": Poem by eight-year-old.

experience and from the other children, the exhilaration of being in and feeling extremes of weather. They learned to cope with wet and cold, began to bring boots to school, and joined the others moaning and groaning when the school authorities decided that, in fact, the weather was too bad for outdoor recess.

Each season brought its own possibilities for exploration and drama on the playground. In the fall, the children continued their usual activities, weather permitting, of digging, rolling logs, play-acting, and so on. They also made exciting new discoveries: seeds in a crack, the last dandelion, fungi "like yoghurt." And, as responsible caretakers, aware of the impending cold weather, they provided houses for worms.

When the temperature dropped below freezing, the appearance and feel of the playground changed dramatically. The edges became hard, the dominant colors changed from shades of green and brown to black, gray, and white. The children kept warm by chasing one another, sliding, breaking up ice formations, throwing snowballs, and performing feats of physical skill (like running along the snowy ridge). As in the fall and spring, they were involved in projects of construction and engineering— digging tunnels, building bridges, moving logs.

Then, after the months of cold, spring brought warmth, greenery, and living creatures. Many cultures have myths explaining the miracle of spring. In Greek mythology, winter was created when Demeter, goddess of the harvest and grain, mourned the loss of her daughter, Persephone, kidnapped by Hades, god of the Underworld. In her grief, Demeter plunged the world into barren, cold winter. Through the intervention of Zeus, an agreement was reached whereby Persephone was returned annually to her mother for 6 months. Demeter expressed her joy at this reunion by returning to the world warmth, bright colors, and growing things—the miracle of spring. The children, who had studied ancient Greece (one of the recurring subjects for the winter curriculum, "Long Ago and Far Away"), were familiar with this story.

On the playground, the children rushed about, expressing their new sense of freedom. They also, however, took time to attend to nature and its many small miracles: the appearance of bulbs planted months before and mostly forgotten in the interim, buds on trees, the sprouting of unseen seeds in unlikely places. All these were causes for wonder and delight.

Natural materials along with hardy flowers—dandelions, buttercups, butter-and-eggs—became props for play-acting, with form suggesting function, or vice versa. It is difficult to know whether the form of a particular fragment of bark suggested a cell phone to Lizzie or whether she needed to invent a cell phone and adapted the fragment to meet that need. Did the "large leaf" suggest itself as "shade stuff," or had the children already been looking for something to provide shade for their fairy house?

Dandelions, those small, heroic survivors on sidewalks and vacant lots, miracles in their own way, were appreciated by the children as much as the rarer, cultivated species—no horticultural snobbism here. Dandelions are ubiquitous and tough, also bright and decorative. They were used in many time-tested ways: woven into necklaces, curls made by the stems being split and then dampened with saliva, and, when finally gone to seed, the "clocks," almost as light as air, were blown off. One fall, a dandelion, like "the last rose of summer" was found to be the sole surviving flower on the playground.

Not all the plant life was there, though, by accident. Some was there by intention. The children and teachers collaborated in planting flowers, vegetables, and even trees. The school had space in a community garden across the street where they planted both flowers and vegetables. Unlike the natural growth, these required ongoing care. We will never know, unfortunately, if Jai's "chemical" had any effect in speeding their development.

Houses and other kinds of shelters and "contraptions" were built in protected places around the playground. Beth noted that "house-building is a spring thing." As the weather gets warm, flying, crawling, walking, running, and jumping creatures all build some sort of house, nest, or lair in which to raise a new generation. On the playground, boys and girls built and furnished "houses" with the materials at hand, participating, consciously or unconsciously, in the general preparations of nature for new life and the future.

❧ 4 ❧

The Curriculum: "Long Ago and Far Away"

In the years 1997–2001 at the Mission Hill School, the schoolwide curriculum was divided into three periods, each of which was given to an
in-depth study of one subject area. In the fall, it was an area of social
studies (for instance, the struggle for justice, politics and government,
the world of work, or the peopling of America). In the winter, under the
rubric "Long Ago and Far Away," the children studied a great civilization
of the past (ancient China, Greece, Egypt, or the Mayans). In the spring,
the curriculum focused on natural and physical science.

Each of these schoolwide subjects engaged the children imaginatively and intellectually, with carryover often evident on the playground.
The following excerpts from Beth's column are from a period when the
central curriculum was ancient Egypt.

> What do children of varying ages think about Egypt as they grapple
> with the notion of ancient civilization? An 8-year-old asked: "Are
> they old? How did they fight if they were old? How could the
> pharaoh die if he was guarded? I thought they protect him. If they
> didn't have cars, how come they can have cars now?"
>
> An 8-year-old asked, "How could the pharaoh die if he was the
> sun? We still have the sun."
>
> A child, responding to the question, "If you went to Egypt today,
> would you see any pyramids or statues?"—"I don't think I have
> time today. Maybe I'd have time over the weekend."
>
> A child, responding to the question, "How do we know the ancient
> Nile people really existed?": "Because they told their children and
> their children told their children and they told us . . . and they're
> still talking about it."
>
> Two boys made excavations in the hole: "Pretend it was King Tut's
> tomb." "We have to get the jewels." "I'm going to get the rope [a

Seven-year-old's intricate drawing inspired by schoolwide,
in-depth study of Egypt.

shoelace] to carry the thing out." A girl came up. "Where's the
mummy?" she asked. "By the jewels. Can you not see?"

[A teacher] and a group of older children decided to see if they
could simulate the ancient Egyptians' method for hauling stone
to make the pyramids. They collected logs, put a long-abandoned

blackboard [left from the old high school] over them, and tied cement blocks together on the blackboard. They pulled and pulled, and the mass slowly moved. Then they moved logs from the back to the front for the next bit of progress. "Not easy," they said.

[Examining worm tunnels on the trunk of a tree]: "It looks like hieroglyphics. Let's cut it out and study them to see if they are hieroglyphics."

For some children the tree was a time machine: "We're going back in time." "Put your hand here [a fold in the tree trunk], say your magic number: 3,000 years B.C. and Egypt."

Death continues to fascinate the children. One day a group rolled large leaves into cigar shapes and carried them to the "pyramid" where the salamander mummy is buried. "We found three dead animals—a bee, a moth, and a worm. We are burying them in the pyramid."

"Log runners, log runners," children call as they roll a heavy stone on logs to move it. "Like making the pyramids."

"We are a team of cats and dogs and a team of crocodiles and alligators (pointing to the walkway and steps), and that's the Nile. Figure out who is the messenger."

The children became immersed in these civilizations—ancient Egyptian, Greek, Chinese, and Mayan—through reading, creative work, dramatic productions, discussions, field trips, presentations—immersed intellectually, aesthetically, imaginatively, physically, and emotionally.

Inside the school building, they simulated artifacts and structures and acted out myths and stories. They built models of Egyptian or Mayan pyramids, wrote their names in Chinese characters and their ages in Roman numerals.

The following paragraphs are from a news article in "The Mission Hill School News," April 26, 1999. They describe the culmination of the Egyptian study, an event attended by the whole-school community and parents:

Some students . . . put on an Egyptian puppet show, while others wore and displayed costumes of the old gods and goddesses, and displayed and explained their stories, poems, and research work.

2\9\03

My topic is Egypt so my partner
and I are making a model of
part of the Nile River. It goes
through a town called Giza. I
have a lot of questions about
Ancient Egypt but my main question
is why is the Nile River important?
because thats where the Ancient
Egyptians got their food, like fish.
Also they goot their bath water and
water to drink and for making bread.

Water was important to the
Ancient Egyptians because it only
rained once a year.

The Nile River is the longest
river in the world. It is 1,145
miles long. The Nile flows north-
ward from Lake Victoria into the
Mediterranean sea.

If I was born back when the
Ancient Egyptians were born
I would swim in the Nile River.

"Egypt": Nine-year-old's writing assignment for schoolwide study.

[Kindergarten] students recited two poems they've worked on: "Books to the Ceiling" and "I can." The room was filled with "documentation panels" and "finales" on the Egyptian and Nubian projects the children have engaged in.

At the end of the east wing sat a grand Egyptian felucca—a boat that the [children] worked on with [a carpenter, a "friend" of the school]. It was a spectacular experience to apprentice with a real master carpenter. . . . In [another kindergarten] room on Thursday night an Egyptologist shared artifacts with families and students. In the hallway outside [the classroom] is a grand wall painting.

The [fifth/sixth-grade class] put together a museum of their work. A walk into the closet revealed King Tut's sarcophagus and mummy. Another display showed students' ideas about how those huge stones could have been lifted to make pyramids.

At the other end of the hallway [second/third graders] presented three skits about Egyptian gods and goddesses—Tegnut, Hathor, and Ra, and ended their performance with a marvelous group dance to Egyptian music. They also shared Egyptian food and three months of work.

[A second/third-grade class] . . . presented two plays: one, "Along the Nile" (about a family's life), was written by students, and the other was adapted from "Pepi and the Secret Names." Families also admired reports and projects that students have worked on all winter.

[A fourth/fifth grade class] displayed their marvelous research reports, as well as the huge and magnificent murals that will eventually line the walls of their basement "tomb." . . . They combined fidelity to the spirit of Egyptian art with the spirit of their own lives and dreams.

[Another fourth/fifth-grade class] performed a musical play they created, based on the book, "Senefer."

Each cultural study took up the winter months and was repeated 4 years later with new materials added by the teachers. Deborah Meier wrote, in the school newsletter, March 12, 1998, "As we decide on the four 'Long Ago and Far Away' topics for our eight-year curriculum, we want to be sure to choose cultures about which lots of resources are available including material that children of different ages will enjoy." The intensity of the children's involvement in the central themes of the curriculum attests to the wisdom of these choices: The themes spilled over onto the playground, where new information, ideas, and vocabulary derived from the curriculum were integrated into imaginative play.

A year later, in April 1999, Meier wrote, "The ancient Nile valley poses a problem when it comes to confirmed facts. It all happened more than two thousand years ago! Much of the evidence is missing and what evidence we do have is open to interpretation—filling in the missing pieces. And some of our kids, after all, are still struggling to make sense of what yesterday means." Children at the school, from age 5 to age 14, transformed and adapted the "facts," struggling to make sense of the past according to their levels of understanding, the younger ones often unclear about issues of space or time or both ("I don't think I have time today [to go to Egypt]. Maybe I'd have time over the weekend"). With age and experience, misconceptions tended to gradually straighten out. The mixed-age groups helped, older children often setting the younger ones straight on the facts when the latter were confused about word meanings ("You didn't 'get' the tomb, you got the mummy").

Children's natural respect for logic and the school's emphasis on "evidence" provided a framework of intellectual discipline that, over the long term, helped maintain the integrity of the cultures being studied, keeping them from being totally at the mercy of the whims and wishes of the children. Playground observations provide examples of children's down-to-earth, everyday logic applied to their study of ancient Egypt: We know about Egyptian culture because "they told their children and their children told their children . . ." "How could the pharaoh die if he was the sun? We still have the sun?"

Characteristically, however, evidence and logic were frequently and intentionally combined with magical thinking by children of all ages. Facts and fancy coexisted easily when the demands of a particular drama made it desirable ("Say your magic number: 3,000 years B.C. and Egypt").

The thematic winter studies were all selected both for their historic importance and for their appeal to both children and adults. To illustrate our point in some depth, however—how children's play can represent and extend classroom learning—we've cited, above, spontaneous playground activities inspired by the schoolwide study of ancient Egypt. Nothing could be more positive evidence of the educational effectiveness of the curriculum in engaging the children.

Pyramids, crocodiles, mummies, the blue and winding Nile itself, along with many other visual images associated with ancient Egyptian civilization, are singular, vivid, and memorable, familiar to us all. On the playground, these images were given new reality as background for play-acting ("Pretend it was King Tut's tomb") and as inspiration for reenactment of ancient procedures (". . . like making the pyramids").

Visual images can serve as instantaneous links transcending time and distance and giving immediacy to events from long ago and far away. A mental image of a pyramid conjures up not only a landscape but an entire culture. Imagination, by definition, is the making of images, and imagination was actively at work as children enriched their outdoor play with what they had learned indoors in the classrooms.

In "The Pedagogy of the Imagination," the English educator Michael Armstrong (2009) assigned to imagination (image-making) a central role in education: "The imagination is fundamental to education in a variety of ways. Firstly, imaginative work is both an embodiment of children's knowledge and the means to its advancement" (p. 48). The Mission Hill children's imaginative play around Egyptian themes "embodied" their new knowledge—of a culture thousands of years in the past—as they re-created artifacts and reenacted rituals.

How, then, did that play advance their knowledge? Learning builds on what is known, and children (and the rest of us) construct new knowledge on a foundation of old knowledge. On the playground, the children used their active imaginations to make connections between their new (and rather esoteric) knowledge about ancient Egypt and their own lives and experiences in urban Boston. One can speculate, for example, that they already had some knowledge of death and probably of wakes, funerals, sitting shiva, and other rituals around death. They re-created an Egyptian-type ritual with mummies and pyramid, connecting what they already knew (had directly or indirectly experienced) with what they had recently learned. ("We found three dead animals—a bee, a moth, and a worm. We are burying them in the pyramid.") In this process, the children advanced their knowledge by grasping on a deep, personal level the meaning of Egyptian rituals and ceremonies to do with mourning and loss.

The spillover of the curriculum onto the playground signified a breakdown in the usual school dichotomy between work and play: Work is characterized as difficult, mental, not fun, imposed by adults, boring; play, as easy, physical, fun, child-initiated, and spontaneous. As the children were reenacting elements and themes of Egyptian culture outdoors on the playground, related activities were taking place indoors: One year, the Nile, made in-scale of blue plastic, curved and irregular, ran 50 feet down the hall floor—the playful invention of a teacher. Walking down the hall, children and teachers skirted its banks, sometimes "waded" through it, or ignored it. The children themselves created models, dioramas, paintings, and costumes, and they wrote and produced plays. Engagement, fun, child-initiated activities—and learning—happened both indoors and out, even if not always evenly distributed (some "work," like lists of spelling words—such as *pyramid*—was academic and not much fun).

In spite of evidence to the contrary, children still think of work as dry and boring. That's what it's "supposed to be"—just as, when playing school, children still turn to 19th-century images of lined-up desks, teach-ers as tyrants distributing punishments, dunces stood up in the corner. Thinking of the curriculum as fun can be confusing for both parents and students, particularly those new to the school. It's "not supposed to be fun." Things that are fun are not deemed serious. A more realistic and complex understanding of both work and play may be part of the educa-tional responsibility of progressive schools—a subject up for both exami-nation and discussion.

PART II

Aspects of Play

The opportunities and responsibilities of public education include preparing children for active, participatory citizenship in a democracy. In our view, this includes encouraging them to become independent thinkers, take intellectual chances, exercise their imaginations, and indulge in creative "wishful thinking." For children in school, developing these intellectual habits requires practice in a safe, encouraging environment—both within the school's walls and outside on the playground.

At the Mission Hill School, the adults responsible for overseeing the playground during recess made a conscious effort to cultivate what might be termed a "civil society." Children learned gradually to respect one another and the environment, "take turns," and develop, with the adults' help and support, commonly understood ground rules for behavior.

In more formally structured games like basketball, four-square, and football, which were particularly popular with the older children, the rules of play were preset so the children first had to learn the rules, then follow them. Obeying rules you haven't created is another experience in civil education.

The school, however, located in the middle of a major city, is not immune to the influences of the surrounding culture, the negative as well as positive ones. The relatively free, creative, and safe environment of the playground is, like all urban playgrounds, vulnerable to the usual social ills—prejudice, stereotyping, cliquishness—and also to the pervasive, often negative, influence of the media.

Part II, then, takes up issues on the playground having to do with creating an ethical, safe, educationally worthwhile context for play. Chapter 5 contains a rationale for educating children to participate responsibly in a democratic society. Chapter 6 relates how agreement on rules, basic order, and mutual respect developed as the playground culture. Chapter 7 discusses the role of games, both formal and informal, in helping children learn to "play by the rules." The last two chapters are concerned with some of the potentially difficult social issues encountered on the playground, issues that presented some threat to the ongoing peaceable, civil culture: Chapter 8 concerns issues of age, gender, and race; Chapter 9, the culture of violence encouraged by the popular media. These two last chapters relate how these problematic aspects of society were encountered and dealt with by adults and children on the playground.

↬ 5 ↫

"Wishful Thinking"

CHANGES IN CHILDHOOD

Once upon a time, before education was mandated and became a public responsibility, children witnessed and participated closely in the daily life of home and community. In the process, they developed some understanding of how things worked in the adult world—from the concrete, physical experiences of starting a fire, drawing water, or spinning yarn to the more distant and general rules governing family authority, relationships, and community responsibilities. Children's lives then, though integrally involved in the adult world, were, of course, far from ideal. Their families suffered from multiple hardships and deprivations, and child labor was an essential part of the economy.

Most of us would not trade those times for ours. Nonetheless, some aspects of modern life bring different kinds of deprivations for children as they spend less time in the company of adults and participate less in useful domestic tasks or social community. Their lives are increasingly filled with virtual realities. Children spend long hours sitting in front of TV screens seeing moving images of a created world when they have barely had a chance to experience, or explore firsthand, the real one. The basic elements of education—a feel for the surrounding physical and social/political structures—have been bypassed. There is little space, time, or opportunity for preschool children to experiment and explore; there is little encouragement to invent, envision other worlds, exercise creative imagination, even to seriously think. Nor do the toys children are given encourage invention or imagination; most have limited possibilities and are designed to develop specific skills or abilities judged necessary for school success. Thus, most children arrive in elementary school without the kind of knowledge we believe furthers the development of strong, independent learners and future members of a democratic society.

EDUCATION AND DEMOCRACY

In view of human history, the idea of a democratic society may seem at times counterintuitive and naive. In fact, the practice of true democracy still retains some aura of naive idealism, of an unrealistic dream, of "wishful thinking." Democracy rests on unproven assumptions about the ability of ordinary people to govern themselves. Nonetheless, if democracy still seems at times an idealistic dream, better to hope and struggle for it than accept its defeat, better to live by utopian dreams than dystopian nightmares, better to believe in the struggle for a better world than believe it cannot happen.

My (Deborah's) own hopes and ongoing optimism are supported by my experiences as a kindergarten and Head Start teacher in the schools on the South Side of Chicago, in a Head Start center in Philadelphia, and in kindergarten classrooms in Harlem in New York City. Here I found the basis for a renewed conviction that democracy is, at the very least, possible. When 5-year-old Darrell insisted that rocks were indeed "alive" and convinced his classmates that this was so, he was practicing habits that were far more important than the lesson about living versus nonliving things that was the object of my lesson plan. He was "playing with" the quite sophisticated concept of "livingness" and, furthermore, was taking responsibility for his own ideas.

Today, 40 years later, when I revisit these "children's gardens," I find Darrell's kind of imagination and lively independent-mindedness under assault. Thoughtful exchanges with young children depend on a quality of childhood that I assumed was timeless—the serious (and courageous) commitment to ideas. Today, however, in order to continue feeling optimistic about the future of democracy, we find we need to actively protect these qualities of childhood, protect the existence of true "kindergartens" in which young children can play freely with both materials and ideas.

Leaving no time or space in education for children's "playful" efforts to make sense of the world risks the future not only of poetry and science but also of our political liberties. The habits of playfulness in early life are the essential foundations upon which we can build a K–12 education that would foster, nourish, and sustain the apparent "absurdity" of democracy.

THE HABITS OF DEMOCRACY

In this book we show—actually illustrate—how schoolchildren's creative play can contribute in significant ways to their academic and social/political education as they explore together ideas, materials, and relationships. Games—those invented in the moment, inherited through tradition, or directed by a teacher—are also relevant to growth and learning. For instance, children's deep concern with issues of "fairness" has implications for the development and practice of democracy in America. The familiar playground cry "That's not fair!" can evolve from an individual's sense of personal outrage, whether justified or not, to a broader concern with "fairness" for the whole group; then, later on, from the same understanding can come, for example, a deeper appreciation of the causes of the American Revolution.

Looking more analytically at education for democracy in schools brings up a basic, important question: Does a commitment to fairness in an immediate situation extend to a general concept of equity—of fairness for all, not just for those in this place and under these circumstances? We know that the notion of equity has shallow roots in most civilizations with which we are familiar, including our own, and freedom, for which we all yearn, remains a fragile concept open to different interpretations and modifications. The practice of democracy, which depends on fairness, equity, and freedom, is no more stable than these, its foundations. Winston Churchill once said about democracy, "It's a thoroughly flawed and absurd idea," but then added, "until one considers the alternatives."

The continuing viability of democratic institutions can't depend entirely on an established body of laws; it requires, in addition, daily practice—inculcated habits of thought and behavior. These habits can be articulated and intentionally practiced in educational settings.

HABITS OF MIND

At the Mission Hill School, K–8 education was built around a set of habits of mind directed at both academic and nonacademic growth, practiced in the classrooms and outside on the playground.

- Evidence: How do we know what we know? What kind of evidence leads to credibility? Can we trust our senses?
- Viewpoint: Would it look/feel different from a different perspective? How does it appear if one stands in another's shoes?
- Connections/Relevance: Is there a perceptible pattern or connectedness, one that is both aesthetic and/or logical?
- Conjecture: What if . . . ? Could things be otherwise? Supposing that . . . Let's pretend that . . .
- Importance: Who cares? Does it matter? Why is it important?

Watch children at play and these are the questions they are exploring—with the kind of intensity and perseverance few adults display. On the playground, education for democracy is active when children are free to follow their interests and concerns. Children pretend and imagine,

> ## My Evidence
>
> My evidence to prove this is all the evidence I need, but wait a minute what if I rotate this what will happen oh it works it balances thats all the evidence I need, but wait one more minute what if I change the mass oh cool its still the same thats all the evidence I need, but wait another minute I can put an axle on it oh I'm so happy it works thats all the evidence I need, but wait what if I revolve it oh yes it works thats all the evidence I need what ok its time for dinner buy.

Writing by ten-year-old about one of Mission Hill School's "Habits of Mind."

rethink and revise, argue and demonstrate, create and design, negotiate and compromise, laugh and cry, build structures and enact dramas, invent something that pleases them—that works in their terms or in those of their playmates. They are absorbed and focused, often open-minded and empathetic. All the crucial habits of mind are being developed as they are "played out."

The future of democracy, in my view, depends on "wishful thinking" in the positive sense, on playing with ideas and being able to imagine better solutions. As adults, we need to cultivate the habit of taking leaps beyond our own self-interest and kinship. It is from such thinking that new realities are invented. If we close ourselves off to the possibility that rocks might be alive, we will lose those opportunities and likely, with them, democracy itself.

❧ 6 ❧

Laws, Rules, and Understandings

NATURAL AND SOCIAL LAWS

There are two kinds of laws governing our lives: natural, scientific laws that underlie the behavior of the physical world and social laws constructed by people to control human impulses and make community life possible. Children are deeply interested in both. They observe and investigate the laws of nature, noting how leaves change color in the fall, experimenting with the slipperiness of ice, watching the circle of waves expand after a pebble is dropped in water. They also recognize and ordinarily accept the social laws that form the basis for the rules of conduct on the playground. They turn to rules to set guidelines for games and to settle disputes.

Children create and invoke rules mainly to set guidelines for games and settle disputes. Adults have broader, though overlapping, purposes for setting rules, stemming from their responsibility for the general physical and emotional safety of the children on the playground. Sometimes rules are negotiated with children, sometimes stated by adults on their own authority. We begin this chapter with children's own ways of rule-making, then turn to Beth's experience as one of the responsible adults present on the playground.

> "Jamie's the lady. I told her to be. I made up the game." "No, me and my brother already know how to play cops and robbers." "But this cops and robbers is a different game." "But there can be two ladies." "No, there can't." "There are two detectives." "I'm the robber. Now you go somewhere and be a second lady."

> Dog catcher is a game that sometimes causes arguments too. "We can change into different kinds of animals." "But we have to play by the rules." "I want to play castle." "We can have a dog catcher in a castle."

> Arguments about sharing the wagon: "Did you know how we solved taking turns?" asked Amy. "We used the blue circle and each person has a turn around the circle."

"But we were there first!" has been the cry from the lilac bushes where planks, logs, and the small parachute are used to make a house. "But we built it and now you've taken it to pieces." "No, the after-school did that." "We need it for our clubhouse."

There have been real problems to think about. Isaac did not want to be the Bad guy in Star Wars again. Max said, "But we have to have a Bad Guy. We are all Good Guys." The bell to go in solved this problem today. And what about Carol not wanting to be "it" in a game of tag?

There were problems on two days: what happens when one child does not want to be an animal or a family member? Most of the time these problems are resolved without adult help, but some-times they produce tears and no one plays. One day when they couldn't agree on a game, children practiced climbing, balancing, and jumping.

In their imaginative play, it could be said that children are working out social rules and relationships. In the above examples of playground disputes, along with their solutions or frustrated stalemates, one can begin to see the evolution of a "civil society"—children trying to work things out. Sigmund Freud (1930/1961), in *Civilization and Its Discontents*, saw civilization as a giving up of innate, basic human impulses in favor of the survival of society. The children on the playground were negotiating, ar-guing, giving up self-interest and controlling impulses, often reluctantly, in order to save the game and, more broadly, be able to live together. It was not easy and didn't always work out; occasionally there were hard feelings and tears.

Children's solutions to social problems were sometimes ingenious, sometimes fragile: improvisations (having a "second lady" or a "dog catcher in the castle"), questionable legalistic claims ("We were there first"), stated needs ("We need a clubhouse"), generally accepted principles (taking turns) and, of course, playing by the rules. Some of these represented assertions of self, others, the more rational solutions, were relatively "de-centered"—generalized agreements that approach the status of rules. All these rationalizations, of course, are also familiar in adult society.

In formal games, there is little opportunity for argument: The rules are already established, written down somewhere. In informal games like jump rope or tag, rules are made partly through precedent and partly through on-the-spot improvisation. Children argue and negotiate and, in fact, often spend just as much or more time establishing the rules as playing by them.

In imaginative play, children's engagement in rule-making is even looser and somewhat resembles the work of scientists experimenting, discovering, remembering, and ultimately, perhaps, reaching generalizations. The children tried out, and speculated about, interpersonal relationships: What are the assumptions behind sisterhood and motherhood? Is family loyalty a "must" and, in betraying it, is one breaking a social rule?

FAIRNESS

There are, however, some principles or tacit agreements behind the rules children invoke. "Fairness" and its derivative "reciprocity" (less often invoked) are akin to universal laws: They are understood and consented to by all even though, in specific instances, there may be disagreement about an application. The practice of "fairness" protects the rights of the individual or minority group in the face of superior power (and it is, of course, the abrogation of such rights in the larger world that can lead to the demise of democracy and the establishment of dictatorships). Though they may argue about the interpretation of fairness in a given situation, children rarely question its basic value or "rightness." Like law, it has the authority of generality and permanence. "Reciprocity" is a form of "fairness" in two-party relationships: "If I invite you to my birthday party, you have to invite me to yours."

TRADITION AND LORE

In addition to "fairness," rules also depend on tradition and cultural lore. The way things have been done in the past is a persuasive, though not always a conclusive, rationale for how they should continue to be done. Vygotsky gives an account of two real sisters "playing sisters," a game in which they keep reminding each other that sisters are "supposed" to be nice to and care for each other. Assertions like "Sisters don't . . ." or "Mothers are supposed to . . ." or even "We have to have a Bad Guy"—all invoke the authority of precedent. There are culturally based assumptions, also, behind the roles of bus driver, explorer, or schoolteacher.

PLAYING AND REALITY

A further constraining influence on the understandings around play is its relationship to reality. There seems to be an agreement among children not to stray too far from the familiar structures and organization of the real world. Play can and does involve fairies, spaceships, wild beasts, and outer space, but the fairies resemble ordinary people, the spaceships are organized like houses, the beasts live in familiar domestic arrangements, and other planets turn out to be much like our own. This is probably due not so much to lack of inventiveness on the part of the players but rather to one of the aims of imaginative play, which is to test the familiar, everyday world, not to create a ruleless world without predictable patterns. Creating a parallel world gives children the freedom to test social rules and assumptions through dramatic reenactments in a novel context— rabbits, rather than children, disobeying their mother.

The criteria behind the rules established on the playground bear a relationship to the habits of mind promoted at the Mission Hill School, habits that, as we've mentioned earlier, the school believes to be necessary for all intellectually serious activity: evidence, viewpoint, connections/relevance, conjecture, and importance. Undirected, children experienced how these abstractions actually "play out": What was the evidence (that the "after-school took it [the house] to pieces?")? Was one viewpoint sufficiently authoritative ("I made up the game")? Was the claim "We have to play by the rules?" also relevant to life off the playground? Regarding conjecture, what happens if no one wants to be "it"? The fifth habit of mind, importance, may, in fact, not have come up spontaneously on the playground, importance being perhaps more important to teachers than to children.

Children seek safety in rules—protection from one another and from potential chaos. If at times they rebel, reinterpret, change, or recklessly break the rules, ultimately they depend on them to lend order and a degree of security to their lives. Natural laws imply a stable universe. Social laws enable a livable society. Children sense the need for both.

In the following pages, Beth describes her experience negotiating rules with children—or sometimes proclaiming them herself—in order to make the playground a safe, positive environment for creative play.

OBSERVING PLAY

I [Beth] wanted to be present at play time to help make it a valuable time for all and, by observing the children, to get to know them better and share my observations with teachers. I was outside with kindergartners through fifth graders the first year and eventually, as the school grew, with kindergartners through eighth graders. The kindergartners through fourth graders tended to gravitate to the grassy areas, while the 10- to 12-year-olds played ball games and jump rope on the hardtop—although they, too, from time to time, climbed on the tree and played under the lilacs.

I, along with student teachers and aides, supervised the grassy parts of the playground. I knew from experience it would take careful observation and planning as well as continuous negotiation with children to develop a play-area culture that would keep children safe but also free to invent their own games.

During the first days of school, the children ran around wildly, some falling and skinning knees on the steps or falling off the tree. There was a lot of crying. So, we met—children and adults—and talked about the fact that some children were being hurt and frightened and that the school was responsible for the safety of all. What should we do? Everyone agreed that pushing people over or hitting was wrong. I pointed out that it was often difficult in an exciting chase not to push or hit and that people were likely to get hurt, especially when there were walls to bump into and other children playing on the steps and under the tree. A few children, who had fallen, thought that chasing games were dangerous. I said that, since there was not enough room on the grassy areas for chasing games and that, though children could run up and down the slope, chasing games should be kept to the hardtop. Though several boys objected, claiming that chasing was fun, gradually, as they became involved in projects and imaginative play, they confined chasing games to the hardtop. At the beginning of each schoolyear, new students often needed to have this understanding explained to them. Everyone agreed, when we met together from time to time, that play time should be fun for all and that adults shared responsibility for making this possible.

As problems arose over the years, as they inevitably do when large groups are together in a limited area, we would meet with the children involved in a particular dispute and talk about what to do. Sometimes I laid out rules in response to a particular situation; sometimes children recognized the need for a general rule. There were problems, for instance, with jump ropes: A child was tied up with a rope because a hunter had caught a wild animal; the police caught a dangerous robber and tied him up; a horse needed rope reins in order to gallop around; a rope tied to a branch was a swing. Using jump ropes in these ways was clearly dangerous. When no children agreed, I asserted my authority, reminding them that adults were responsible for their safety and that ropes were to be used only for jumping.

CHILDREN INITIATING RULES

Sometimes the children took the initiative in setting limits. The care of
the lilac tree, overhanging the wall above the hardtop, was an early concern. The children loved to swing on it and drop down. One day when
a child was swinging, a branch broke. Children who had been playing
house under the tree were angry and sad and took me to see what had
happened. I showed them the buds on the tips of branches and told them
these would be flowers in the spring if no more branches were broken.
So another rule was made, this time by the children—no climbing on the
lilac tree. Children enforced this rule vigorously. When the tree flowered
in May, children shouted, "Come and see." When a child would climb on
the lilac in the winter, another would tell her to get down because the
tree would have flowers in the spring.

We worked together to develop a play-area culture based partly on
children's implicit sense of fairness. When children began to dig a hole near
the fence, using hoes, shovels, and rakes that had been bought for garden-
ing, arguments arose about who could use them. It was obvious that there
were not enough tools (or space) at one time for everyone who wanted to
dig. Some tried to wrest tools from others. Children complained that other
children did not allow them a turn. The boys who started the hole thought
they should be the only ones to dig. Again, we met and I asked, "What
should we do?" "Take turns" came from a chorus of children. "But how?"
After some disagreements and angry pulling away of tools, we agreed that
those who wanted to dig each play time should have a chance. If all the
shovels were in use, other children should stand by and wait to take a turn.
It was agreed that, to avoid accidents, hoes and shovels should not be raised
more than shoulder-high. During these discussions, the digging stopped; it
usually resumed without any more problems.

EMOTIONAL SAFETY

In addition to protection from physical dangers, children sometimes
needed protection from emotional stress. In the first months of school,
older children made fun of some of the younger children's play: "Don't
you know a unicorn is not real?" The older children needed to learn what
it was like to "walk in someone else's shoes," which, with practice and the
occasional intervention of adults, they gradually did learn. Understanding
another's point of view is a principle of both the indoor and outdoor cultures at the Mission Hill School, one of the five habits of mind. Over time,

this view was absorbed; there were fewer and fewer examples of hurtful words or sudden bursts of anger.

CHILDREN AS OBSERVERS

During play times, I wandered around with a little notebook taking notes on what the children were doing and saying so I could share events with the staff. In the second semester of the first schoolyear, I began to write a weekly article based on these notes for the newsletter that was sent to parents and friends. I wanted others to see the developmental value of play time for learning and to share the delight of observing what the children imagined and invented. Often children followed me and asked what I was writing. I told them I wrote in order to remember what they did. Sometimes a child wanted to write in my book, and sometimes a child brought out a notebook of her own and wrote in it; sometimes a child would come to me and say, "Write this down; it is interesting" or "Come with me and see what we found." Children took great interest in what others were doing and often began a similar game or asked to join in. Beginning in the second year, several older children (ages 10 to 12) took over my note-taking on some days and even wrote the articles for the weekly newsletter.

Older children who did not want to play organized games on the hardtop wandered around with me, talking about what we were observing and the things that interested them. Some of these children became close observers. I was called frequently to "See this" or "See what I can do" or "See what _____ can do."

ESTABLISHING A PLAYGROUND CULTURE

We all grew close, and children knew they had friends who would join them in their pretend play when mud could be soup, and a wall a motorcycle, a leaf a baby, and the beech tree a beloved creature to be hugged or a monster to be feared. They also knew they were free to explore and to ask what something was and to question other children: "What are you doing?" and "Can I play?"

Over the years, the children grew in their ability to play and work together. Children and adults built a community of trust, negotiating rules for safety and fairness. I saw the children develop respect for one another's play, accomplishments, interests, and differences. They were, of course, learning to do this in the classrooms, too, but on the playground an observer could more easily stand back and watch how individuals and groups of children of different ages responded to physical, intellectual, and social challenges.

The school's unkempt, messy (to adult eyes) playground provided opportunities not offered in typical playgrounds with swings, slides, and climbing frames—all permanent structures that, although they can be enjoyed, don't easily lend themselves to imaginative transformations. It is important to emphasize, however, that this positive experience outside at recess did not just happen—it was the result of a conscious effort to work with the children to establish an environment that gave them the freedom to invent and explore and at the same time feel safe and supported.

♫ 7 ♪

Playing Games

ON THE HARDTOP

Every recess, children poured out of the school building onto the playground, lined up, and waited for Mr. S. [assistant principal] to announce the available options and lay out the general parameters for the day. These might be "girls basketball," a new game to be learned, or a piece of equipment to be tried (e.g., stilts made of inverted buckets with rope handles); also, the children were cautioned about potential hazards—the grass too soggy to play on, the basketball court slippery with ice. Eager to get on with the activities, the children could be impatient with explanations and announcements and sometimes had to be reminded to listen, which resulted in the announcements taking longer than anyone wanted.

When released, the children fanned out, sorting themselves into the different areas according to choice of activity, the entire outdoor space suddenly alive with sound and motion. The kind of fantasy play described in Part I usually took place in the grassy areas, around the bushes or the tree. Those who wanted to use the various pieces of available equipment or play more formally organized "games" gravitated towards the hard-surfaced areas, where there were always two or more adults supervising, instructing, or actively participating in the play—usually the assistant principal and Lukas, an all-round aide, joined at various times by other staff members or interns.

Most of the time Beth chose to stay in the softer, greener areas, where she was close enough to the action to record, in some detail, the children's words and at times, on invitation, take part in their play. Meanwhile, though, a lot was happening on the hardtop—physical feats, skills practice, and a variety of organized games. Beth's notes and observations of these activities are more summary, the view more distant. We know from her weekly columns the nature of the social groupings and activities on the hardtop, but, because the words are missing, we don't have the same glimpses into the children's inner lives—their feelings, ambitions and motivations. It is important, nonetheless, to describe what children actually were doing in the hardtop area in order to give a full picture of the activities on the playground at recess time.

Hardtop area of playground.

To begin with, invention and imagination were at work everywhere—
though in less obvious ways on the hardtop. Imaginative input here
seems to have been of a different kind from that on the grassy areas—
less fantasy, less imagining oneself into another person, creature, or
thing; more improvisation, adjustment to circumstances, and invention
of new kinds of games and physical challenges. On the other hand, we
have no way of knowing whether a child shooting baskets was imagining
himself as Kareem Abdul-Jabbar or Larry Bird or, handling a football, as
Peyton Manning or Randy Moss. It is quite possible some children had
heroic images in their heads that subtly influenced their poses, gestures,
and behavior.

Watching a local sandlot baseball game recently, I [Brenda] recognized the home-team pitcher's silent, intent, and motionless stance on the mound before going into action to deliver the pitch: upper body leaning forward and swiveled toward home plate, bent wrist of hand holding ball resting on back of hip, cap pulled down shadowing the eyes, a piercing gaze directed toward the batter. The pose was familiar from the many times I had seen it assumed by professional major league pitchers. The imitation was uncanny, detail-for-detail. Some children at Mission Hill School, watching sports on TV and occasionally seeing live games, had heroes whom they both emulated and imitated.

Girls at Mission Hill School in those days didn't appear to have images in mind of female sports figures. Though outstanding women athletes like Venus and Serena Williams received a good deal of attention in the media, they weren't on the radar screen of girls at Mission Hill in spite of their professed feminism (demanding, for instance, equal time on the basketball court). In fact, they were more likely to act as cheerleaders on the edge of boys' games or mimic pop singers (like Beyoncé of Destiny's Child), wrapping themselves intimately around a "microphone" (likely a piece of wood or plastic hockey stick).

THE GAMES

Most of the games played on the hardtop areas were organized around geometric lines and shapes painted on the pavement: circles (foot or tricycle races), squares (game of four square), rectangles (basketball, soccer, football, street hockey); also, for more pedagogical purposes, a compass and a map of the United States appeared on the hardtop.

The symmetrical shapes, measured out and marked according to the rules of the games, were often radically altered to fit in the available area. Limitations of space (the playing field was less than half standard length) and sometimes of equipment (broken, missing, or not there in the first place) meant that the parameters of traditional, established sports had to be modified. The result was a good deal of improvisation and negotiation—new rules invented or renegotiated according to circumstances. In spite of necessary adjustments and compromises, the basic structure of conventional ball games was usually (though not always) recognizable.

Football is the game of the moment with the older children. Four girls join a group of 12 boys for a kind of game I do not understand. The ball goes like a bullet from one person to another but there does not appear to be any goal scoring. There is no touching, just running and passing.

Hockey continues to attract boys and girls of all ages. Unfortunately, there are three broken sticks without heads, but that doesn't keep players from using them anyway. It is impressive to see children going after the ball with only a straight, headless stick.

Some areas of hardtop remained unmarked and open to other kinds of games and activities: traditional "children's games" with unwritten rules— like jump rope, keep-away, tag, blind man's buff, hide-and-seek—as well as games wholly invented by the children. Without designated boundaries, these were played wherever there was suitable, available space, either on the hardtop or green areas and sometimes ranging across both.

The assistant principal and some of the older boys invented a game [called] soccer wall. The soccer ball is kicked against the wall of the school above a line of bricks. It is allowed to bounce three times only before it is kicked by a different player. The game is a challenge of strength and speed.

A similar invented game, using a tennis ball, was named "wall ball." Innumerable versions of tag were invented or reinvented—freeze tag, elbow tag, leapfrog tag, among others. Children marked squares and rectangles on the pavement with colored chalks for various versions of hopscotch.

During a period designated as "gym time" (distinct from recess), which took place either in an undersized indoor gym or outdoors, new games were introduced by staff members: red-light-green-light, dodge ball, sharks-and-minnows, and others. These games were then taken on by the children on the playground.

Initiated by the children, jump rope, stepping games, and clapping games were particularly popular among girls. Accompanying rhymes and chants were mostly hand-me-downs from the past and often from other countries. The following chants were recalled later by several of the children who had participated in the games:

> Cinderella dressed in yella
> Went up stairs to kiss her fella
> By mistake she kissed a snake
> How many doctors did it take?
> 1, 2, 3, 4 . . .

Strawberry shortcake,
Blueberry pie,
Who's going to be your lucky guy?
A, B, C, D . . . (or boys' names)

Handclap rhymes:

Miss Mary Mack, mack, mack
All dressed in Black, black, black
With silver buttons buttons, buttons
All down her back back back
She asked her mother, mother, mother
For fifteen cents, cents, cents
To watch the elephants, elephants, elephants
Jump over the fence, fence, fence
Jumped so high, high, high,
They reached the sky, sky, sky
And didn't come down, down, down
'til the 4th of July!

Oh I won't go to [place] anymore, more, more
There's a big fat policeman at the door, door, door
He'll grab me by the collar, and make me pay a dollar,
So I won't go to [place] anymore, more, more

CHOICES

Children's choices of what to play, which games or sports, were influenced by a number of considerations: what was "going on," the equipment available, novelty, the weather, friendship groups, the presence of
adult coaches/participants, and, finally, those mysterious fads and fashions that cause a game to be hugely popular for a period until it loses appeal and another takes its place.

The school provided equipment for a great variety of organized games
and other activities: balls, Frisbees, rackets, bats, hockey sticks, basketball
hoops, goals, tricycles, wagons, jump ropes, and miscellaneous toys. The
equipment, of course, was frequently broken and balls lost. In an interview,
Lukas recalled "the shouts of joy when a neighbor on the other side of the
playground wall ventured out in her backyard and proceeded to throw the
balls she found back over the fence—a missing ball meant we couldn't play
a certain game." At times he himself did a "sweep" before recess, "knocking
on the doors of neighbors to collect missing balls."

By Wednesday there were two games of four square, a game of basketball, a game of kickball, a game of soccer, running on the track—
and the little red wagon going round and round.

The second basketball hoop is up and in use. The games . . . are
intense and joyful. Kickball, four-square, tennis [on the days Joyce
was there], and catch with balls of all sizes are also popular.

The greatest excitement for the 6th grade boys was the arrival of
two red trikes that [the assistant principal] put together. The oldest
boys were first to ride them and the first to tip over! There is also
another red wagon put together by Albi and Barry, and a small
wheelbarrow.

The little red wagon goes around now with one passenger as a
precaution against the handle breaking again. Another loss occurred
over the weekend: one of the basketball hoops was destroyed.

There is a new fence on the side of the kickball court to prevent the
balls from going into the parking area.

The arrival of the basketball net was the highlight of the week.
On the first few days there were long lines for shooting. By the
end of the week there were six to eight children in two teams playing with [the assistant principal] or Lukas.

Novelty—fresh ideas, challenges, and new skills to be learned—
influenced the children's choices.

This week the school received some new "toys" for the outside:
high bouncing balls, two small footballs, a riding ball (probably with
a name well known to everyone but me), a balancing disk, and a
marvelous two-person apparatus that requires coordination to send
a ball back and forth on double strings. It is wonderful to see the
delight these objects give the children.

Four-Square is the new game of the week, requiring ball skills, pa-
tience, taking turns. A ball trailing a comet's tail, thrown back and
forth, is the new toy of the week.

Kickball with Lukas has become more popular. Yo-yos are in fashion. "I learned from watching Bennie," said Barry.

Goals have taken the places of the hoops and children of all ages are playing hockey with light plastic sticks and a soft ball. Thomas [aide] and [the assistant principal] are the instructors and referees.

Games on the hardtop continue, but, as one child said, "Dodge ball has lost its flavor."

Weather had a frequent (though not always determining) influence on the choice of games on the playground. Low temperatures encouraged heightened activity. Cold, rain, snow, or wind made certain kinds of games difficult or impossible. Once, after a snow and with snowball-throwing forbidden, a staff member drew a chalk target on the wall of the building; this worked as an effective substitute for human targets. On another occasion, students carved out, with shovels, a huge "MHS" on the snow-covered pavement, which they were then delighted to look down on from a second-floor window.

The cold wind blew and the children ran. Football, kickball against the walls of the school, chasing games with animals and raiders and good and bad guys were the games of the week for most of the children.

There's a sheet of ice on the basketball court. The children threw snowballs onto the ice.

The basketball area finally melted in the rains of the weekend and children could shoot baskets again.

On clear days basketball, kickball, four-square, and double-dutch jump rope have been the activities on the hardtop, which has been resurfaced. The courts have been repainted.

Earth—dirt and rocks; Air—cold and warm winds; Water—rain, snow, and ice. These ancient "elements"—all except Fire—have been the playfellows of the children this week.

Much happens in a week of fine weather. Dodge ball is *the* game; kickball has a few players. One basketball hoop has been repaired and a few children shoot baskets; some play soccer.

The playground has been swept clean. Children fill the hardtop with their games. Great shouts of excitement greet the announcement that they may take their coats off. Games of tag, basketball, kickball, football, and hockey are easier without coats.

Many of the children, particularly the younger ones, tended to move in groups, choosing activities by consensus, often changing in the middle of recess time.

Do the children come outside knowing what they will play, or do the choices friends make steer them, or do they make instant decisions?

Groups of children of different ages run, climb, and jump on the grass and around the tree and lilac bushes. Some groups stay for the entire play time; others race and run and then go to jump rope or join a ball game.

"We've changed from making fairy houses to tag," says an eight-year-old as he races by. "Unfreeze me!" shouts Marisa. "The tree is the base," says Weldon. "Who's it?"

What prompts change in play and groups? Some children tend to be together most playtimes, but others enter and leave the groups, and new groups form for a day or two. Some older children (ages 8 and 9) who used to be involved in imaginative games now play ball games much of the time.

Finally, the presence of skilled adults as both instructors in new skills and models of playful engagement were important factors in choices made.

What causes the popularity of different ball games? This week Helen [staff] played touch football with a group of boys and the group has grown to two games of football with the assistant principal. Priscilla [intern] is a formidable basketball player with both the younger and older children. Lukas has a large group playing kickball every day. And Zelda and Erica [interns] play whatever ball game needs another person.

[One of the assistants in the art room] is a star hockey player. She taught the children how to "bully," that is, cross sticks before a face-off. Even on the coldest day, [she] was outdoors playing hockey with the children.

And Joyce [staff] has begun teaching the children [during periods of electives] to play tennis. They are using the wall of the school to practice. Again, children of all ages want to play.

One day there was a lively game of hide-and-seek on the grass with Amy [intern]. There are not many places to hide, but the young children found people, corners of the building, and places in the tree to hide behind, and there were loud shrieks when Amy found them.

Kala [intern] recited a rhyme as she counted off five children to choose "it" for a game of Blind Man's Bluff.

COMPETITION

Inside the school walls, competition was played down—never, as in many schools, used to motivate academic achievement or good behavior. At Mission Hill School there are no grades or systems of rewards and punishments. Rather, students are encouraged to find the world interesting— worth investigating and learning about. Collaboration, "learning from each other," and group projects are central to the school's pedagogy, with promotion and graduation based on the individual's demonstrated progress toward academic competencies.

On the playground, however, competition is still an organizing principle and motivation in most games. (Some attempts were made by teachers to introduce the children to noncompetitive, cooperative games, but these were not noteworthy—that is, not noted down in the weekly columns.) The games that were commonly played were structured around one or more primary aims with different degrees of competition built in: (1) to demonstrate feats of strength and speed, (2) to practice and show off a skill, and (3) to compete with and win over other individuals or teams.

The invented game of soccer wall, described above, is an example of the first of these—"a challenge of strength and speed" (in Beth's words), though skill and a tinge of competition are also involved. Jump rope, above all a demonstration of coordination, timing, and skill, illustrates the second aim. Jump rope is essentially a "show-off" feat before an audience of actively engaged peers who chant in unison the rhythmic verses and take turns twirling the rope and being jumpers—roughly 80% skill, 20% competition (depending on who's playing). Soccer, basketball, football, and baseball (all team games) aim at a goal, base, or basket, which, if the attempt is successful, results in a score; competition is built in. On the other hand, wherever there was a basket or anything that could pass for one, boys (and occasionally girls) spent literally hours "shooting baskets," an unscored, informal activity that can be seen as skills practice but seemed to be also just plain fun.

Organized, large-group chasing games like hide-and-seek and tag took place wherever there was adequate space and enough willing players. These games were competitive, yes, but the competition diffused among a number of players taking turns being "it" and consequently became perhaps less intense. Also, for some children, being "it" is a desirable distinction while, for others, it's to be avoided, so the aim of the competition is not always clear.

Although most games are competitive to some degree, sports—all sports by definition—end with winners and losers. Teams themselves, though, in addition to being competitive with other teams, are internally collaborative. Part of becoming a successful team involves the players learning to depend on and support their teammates.

Perhaps, in the end, what the players most enjoyed, beyond winning, was the exhilaration of exercising skill, strength, speed, and coordination along with teammates.

> Mission Hill School also has a team of 15 girls who will compete at the Reggie Lewis Center on May 13 in a Double Dutch competition. Two groups of younger and older girls practice in the front hall every Tuesday and Thursday.

> The first-ever Mission Hill School relay team has been formed. The team, composed of 16 children, competed at the Copley Square library on Saturday, April 15. The team spent recess during the week before vacation getting in shape by stretching, running, and leaning how to hand the baton to the next runner. They are coached by Jose [staff].

> A team of girls challenges a team of boys in basketball.

Issues of fairness (discussed earlier) can be exacerbated during intense competition. At times, when the situation became too tense, an adult would stop the game and call for a brief "cooling-off period." The school's relatively unenthusiastic attitude toward winning or losing (except when it came to interschool competitions) tended to make winning or losing less crucial, less an investment of ego and self-esteem. It seems likely that the values of cooperation, teamwork, and mutual appreciation, emphasized inside the building, had some long-term influence on how games were played outside.

There is lately less dispute over fairness, less tension around choosing sides for games. Adults must still sometimes intervene, but far less than two years ago.

There are 6 yellow and 6 orange hockey sticks and teams are quickly formed. Sometimes the choice of color is more important than whether the teams are "fair," one side often having more larger or smaller children.

Kickball is back as a popular game. One day, however, according to one player, there was a "slaughter team." What did that mean? It meant that there were seven on one team and ten on another "because no one wanted to move."

There is a small plastic hoop by the back door, and a group of boys of all ages organize themselves into a game in the small space. Six-foot Vinnie and three-plus-foot Tom play in the same game.

PHYSICAL EXERTION

Some of the outdoor activities consisted of neither fantasy play nor games but of simple strenuous exercise, "letting off steam." According to Lukas, some children, mostly boys, enjoyed sheer physical labor—using shovels to clear snow from the hardtop or rakes to clean up debris. They went about these tasks energetically and with evident pleasure, pleasure presumably derived from feeling their own strength and their bodies working toward a useful and visible accomplishment.

And we should take note again of the few holdouts, those children mentioned in the Introduction ("The Children") who chose not to join in ongoing activities, including games. In the current national focus on childhood obesity, there is growing concern about inactive youth. School personnel at Mission Hill were well aware of potential problems with children who, for some reason, preferred not to join in.

We know exercise helps bodies grow strong. So what do we do about the few children who prefer to read or sit and talk during playtime? Sometimes they can be encouraged to take part in a game. It is easier with the young children who want to be included and often only need an invitation. But should we be concerned when an older child is alone or with one other child day after day, not involved in any group activity? Or is it, as one said to me, "my free time to do what I want?"

Age, Gender, and Race

AGE AND GENDER

Issues around age and gender are closely associated, difficult to consider separately since the relationship between the sexes is age-dependent; it changes as children mature. In kindergarten and the early grades, gender roles are relatively fluid. The younger boys at Mission Hill willingly participated in traditional girl-type play (family dramas and relationships) and girls became caught up in boy-type activities like chasing each other and carrying out daring physical feats—jumping off the beech tree stump or crawling across a narrow board between two walls.

Although differences in behavior between boys and girls were generally less marked in those years, some boys did act according to the traditional stereotype, showing off their strength, playing at "shooting" guns, making motorcycle-revving noises and running around the playground, yelling to each other (creating "sound effects" is often a specialty of young males).

> A group of younger boys move the logs to the top of the grassy hill near the road and set up cannons. They sit astride them and pretend to fire away.

> "We picked up that log together and put it down. We were that strong!"

> "This is my motorcycle," said Jake, astride the wall, with a piece of bark in the post hole of the wall as a steering wheel. "Let me on," said Zoe, climbing on behind him. "Stay back of me. Let this motorcycle fly."

> "I've come over in an airplane," said Jake as he and Kali and Louis buzzed around on "motorbikes."

Girls often took the lead in "nurturing" roles—preparing meals, keeping house, and exploring family relationships.

16-year-old daughters [were] tied to their mothers because they
"stayed out too late . . ."

[Two girls] interrupted their building to take a new five-year-old "to
find a friend to play with."

There are many examples of house play in Chapter 1 that show girls
directing the action and taking the dominant roles. Husbands and fathers
appear in these dramas, sometimes in rather "henpecked" roles ("Go get
your father and tell him it's bedtime"); but they can also be the mainstay
of the family after a mother deserts or the generous parent giving the children "TV's [sic] and games," or a cook (Ari stirring "chocolate homemade
stew").

Even when they typecast the adults into gendered domestic roles, the
children themselves are flexible about who plays male or female parts.
Beth noted that "mothers and fathers tend to rotate roles." Either a boy
or girl might be the one to respond to the invitation, "Who wants to be
the father?"

Although, for interrelated biological and cultural reasons, there
seems to be less gender discrimination among children in the primary
grades, there is gender awareness. The fact that boys and girls play together without self-consciousness doesn't mean they are unaware of gender differences. This point is underlined by the boast cited earlier, "I'm a
girl who likes to do dangerous stuff." With this statement, she is expressing not only pride in liking to do "dangerous stuff" but also pride in her
ability to overcome the limitations of being a girl; she does "dangerous
stuff" in spite of being a girl.

The following instances involved both girls and boys:

Twelve children of mixed ages have been playing a family game
with crying babies a volcano, burning houses, and tornadoes.

Children ages 5 to 9 played a wolf-capturing game that became
intense after several days.

A group of 8-year-old boys and girls who often play ball games
made the tree a spaceship. They looked out on the Earth with "bin-
oculars" (hands held to eyes).

The effort to get the stone out involved 30 or more children at different times. Five-year-olds did their part and learned how to push
the shovel into the ground.

In sum, although younger children (ages 5 to 8) engaged in some stereotypical, gender-related activities on the playground, most of the time self-consciousness about gender did not define or limit their play. Boys and girls played together freely and inventively while negotiating the rules and requirements of the particular game or activity in which they were involved.

Age and growth into middle childhood bring profound changes, along with increased awareness and self-consciousness, in the relationships between boys and girls. The older children engaged in less fantasy play, becoming more interested in formal games with rules and requirements—in spite of periodic, sometimes nostalgic, returns to the activities of their younger selves:

Date 6/5/01

Basket ball basketball

It has dots and Lines. It

bounces high and

feels bumpy. Pass It!

bounce and throw! dribble It

And Shoot it in the basket!

"Basketball": Writing by twelve-year-old girl.

Two older boys rediscover the tree, building and playing on it. "I had forgotten what fun this is," says one as they pretend to be mountain climbers.

"Animal teen-agers" were fed snow in their nests in the corners of the snow walls.

I [Beth] was always fascinated by the fact that [imaginative] games were played by children of mixed ages. The older children entered into the fantasy world with the same intensity as the younger ones.

Though boys and girls continued to play together, participation in certain sports, like football or jump rope, was dominantly by either males or females.

A hockey game had two girls and six boys. Equal numbers of boys and girls play four square, kickball, and tennis together.

Both basketball hoops are up. Fifteen boys and one girl played, five on a team.

[Before the hoops were down] two girls played vigorous basketball with the boys.

Older (seven plus) girls and boys played basketball, hockey, football, and soccer. Only girls jumped rope.

The school staff were eager to break down traditional gender stereotypes: They encouraged girls to play football and boys to jump rope. The methods of encouraging this participation across gender lines, consistent with the school's philosophy and pedagogy, were by example rather than dictum: a male teacher doing double-Dutch rope jumping (probably for the first time in his life!) and female teachers playing football. Some of the older girls, too, self-designated feminists, joined in the boys' games and, on at least one occasion, challenged them competitively.

This week Helen [staff] played touch football with a group of boys.

Will boys begin to jump rope now that Lukas [staff] has joined the double-dutch group?

Kickball with Lukas attracted a large group of children of mixed ages at both playtimes. There was football too.

At the first recess, a few boys shot baskets; at the second, a group of ten took turns shooting baskets and guarding—all boys. It is interesting that when Priscilla [intern] was here, basketball was mixed, boys and girls.

Wonderful news: more girls want to play basketball. But the difficulty is, how do they learn the skills to join the boys who have been playing "forever?" We are working on it.

SEX, SEXISM, AND RACE

There are several areas in which Beth's weekly columns are not informative: flirtatious relationships between the older boys and girls, racist attitudes and/or behavior at all ages, and homophobia. Lack of evidence, though, does not mean nonexistence; common sense and experience tell us otherwise. When groups of girls were described, huddled together on the tree trunk, whispering and giggling, it could be surmised that some of their whisperings had to do with boys, perhaps, for instance, speculations about "who likes whom." Most of the jump-rope and other chants, cited in the Chapter 7 section "The Games," had to do with sexual relationships. Other chants, also reported by children, were on the edge of being risqué:

Fudge, fudge
Call a judge
[name of girl jumping] is having a baby
Her boyfriend's going crazy
How many babies did she have?
1, 2, 3, 4, . . .

Behind the refrigerator
There is a piece of glass
Miss Suzie slipped upon it
And broke her little —
Ass-k me no more questions
I'll tell you no more lies
The boys are in the bathroom
Zipping up their —
Flies are in the country
The bees are in the park
Where the boys and girls are kissing in the
D-A-R-K, D-A-R-K, D-A-R-K—DARK!

Chanting about sexy stuff was OK—the words traditional and public. Conversation, however, about boyfriends, girlfriends, relationship, and sex was private, covert, not "shared" with the adults on the playground for the usual reasons: possibly fear of disapproval, misunderstanding, censure, ridicule, perhaps, though unlikely, even scolding—also the general sense that sex is a private affair. As a result, we have little information.

As to racism, Beth kept a few notes and recollections. The school was consciously, intentionally integrated—both staff and students. The children, coming from different communities in the city, tended, at least initially, to "hang out" with those most familiar to them—for example, a Jamaica Plain group, a Roxbury group, and so on. Because of de facto housing patterns, it followed that those groups were mostly racially defined. The older boys, however, most of them sports enthusiasts, were more focused on who was a good player than on social membership. The younger children did not remain self-segregated; all played together with little apparent awareness of (or care about) racial differences.

As activities developed on the playground—fantasy play, investigations into nature, engineering projects, games—children of all ages began to sort themselves out more by their interests than by their social/racial identities. Also, with Beth's help, the gradual evolution of a playground ethos—including rules about safety, fairness, respect (for all life)—made the playground into a fundamentally nonthreatening environment. Children were less likely to take offensive or defensive postures, including bullying, teasing, and social exclusivity.

We have no recorded information on homophobia—again, not proof that it didn't exist. At various times homophobia became an issue within the school building but evidently not outdoors.

In sum, although there were, at different times and to varying degrees, social and racial alliances and distinctions, these tended to diminish with time. Almost all the activities and many friendships were interracial and Beth recalls, "I never heard any racial taunts or words—none."

❧ 9 ❧

Influence of the Media: TV, Comics, Toys, Films, and Video Games

POPULAR MEDIA

It is impossible to discuss the inspiration for children's play without addressing the ubiquitous media. Children's eyes and ears are wide open to their surroundings, and, given time and space, they tend to reenact in play what they have experienced, even indirectly. Through these reenactments, children are attempting to get a handle on the world around them, consolidating what they know and gaining new knowledge.

For many decades now, the popular media have had a major influence on the content of play, and many kindergarten and elementary school teachers have expressed dismay at its effect, particularly on the incidence of violence in and outside the classroom. Nancy Carlsson-Paige (2008), citing three recent studies in *Taking Back Childhood*, concludes that "starting with the deregulation of children's television in 1984 . . . and continuing apace, kids' play has become far less creative, with children mimicking what they've seen in the media, rather than coming up with it by themselves" (p. 6). Parents, pediatricians, psychologists, educators, and even politicians have become increasingly concerned with the commercialization of play.

In the period 1998–2001, during which Beth Taylor recorded her observations at the Mission Hill School, virtually all the children had access to TV at home. They undoubtedly watched the programs most children watched at that time, involving superheroes and -heroines, villains, power, and magic, along with lots of excitement, action, and violence—and vivid graphics. They were familiar with the TV characters who also turned up in other commercial enterprises such as toys, movies, comics, video and board games. In an early column, Beth posed basic questions:

> I am fascinated by the children's imaginative lives. What do they mean? How much of their play is derivative of what they see on television? Is it good for them to act out pretend violence?

There are no simple answers to these questions in spite of volumes of research. The playground observations themselves, however, may at least shed some light. It is clear that, at Mission Hill, as at other schools, some proportion of the children's play was derived from TV or other forms of popular entertainment.

> Godzilla tried to catch children on Tuesday but had disappeared by Wednesday.

> "He's invisible. He's covering the world with green. How can we stop him?"

> Monsters were dangerous: "There's a monster. Let's sneak by him to get some food."

> A kind of Pokémon game engages five boys: "I got an idea. Maybe if we play dead, we'll be okay."

Most of these characters and roles are familiar to us: Godzilla has been around for decades and is known to more than one generation of children. We can assume that some traditional "bad guy" or villain is threatening to cover "the world with green." Dangerous monsters are a staple of literature and drama, and Pokémon cards, figures, and animations were familiar at one time to all parents and teachers. The sources for most of the children's recorded imaginative play, however, are not always clear. In fact, characteristically, there are many sources of inspiration—intermixed, invented, rearranged, improvised with the contexts altered.

> "The only way we can settle it is—let me build a time machine so we can go back and see what really happened."

> On the tree: "She's an alien. If you pat her on the back, she won't bite."

> Others played at being aliens. "Look!" said one, holding a leaf wrapped around a wood chip. "I've got a baby alien in there."

> "Put me in the memory box so it connects to my brain."

"Time machines" are a staple of science fiction, but using one to settle a playground argument is a new idea. A "pat . . . on the back" is not a traditional treatment for vicious aliens, and "baby aliens" are an altogether unusual phenomenon, their introduction probably due to the popularity of family play. The apparently automatic connection of the "memory box" to the brain is a novel conception. In fact, close observation and recording of children's play may reveal that what appears to be derivative has been significantly transformed by the children in many ways, both characters and situations altered. Characters (power figures, for instance, like Superman, Batman, Spiderman, and Power Rangers) may retain most of their basic attributes but operate in situations that would surprise their creators.

In addition to fiction and fantasy, events reported in the media (like fashion shows) were grist for the children's imaginations, some of them (like courtroom scenes) having also become subjects of TV dramas.

> One day there was a fashion show, with Amy directing five children in how to walk and turn and pose.

> One group of children conducted a pretend trial: Weldon is both witness and lawyer. Bill is both Katie's lawyer and witness.

> "I'm going to do the moonwalk, everybody," said Arnie as he walked on another branch.

LIMITED DIRECT EFFECT OF MEDIA INFLUENCE

In spite of the above examples, play directly derived from commercial characters and programs was reported surprisingly rarely in Beth's newsletter columns, and there were no examples of "scripted play" (where children actually reproduce words and slogans from commercial programs). The task, however, of identifying the subtle influence of the popular media on vocabulary, postures, and events on the playground is nearly impossible. It is interesting and instructive to speculate on the reasons why these children on this playground at this time seemed more involved with fairies, family scenes, the natural environment, and even the school curriculum than with commercial materials aimed specifically at an audience of children. Several tentative explanations come to mind. The one we particularly like is that there were many more interesting possibilities for play than the media-derived, stereotypical figures and dramas.

Beth, in her notes, suggests that "the unkempt naturalness of our grassy play areas encourages imaginative, inventive, and problem-solving activities." There were no jungle gyms or swings or parallel bars. To entertain themselves, the children were virtually forced to invent, and, of course, the opportunities were infinite, everything possible for the active imagination.

Open-ended materials like sand, earth, and water, along with blocks, paints, clay, and paper, have long been the materials of choice for progressive educators. With no narrowly designated uses, possibilities for transformation and novelty are open-ended and inviting. The unformed, messy playground was full of suggestions and invitations to the imagination. When the children poured outdoors at recess, the raw materials on the playground were instantly and enthusiastically transformed by them into, for instance, dramatic props (dried leaves became dishes; a tree branch, a horse), scenery (fairy houses in the lilac bushes), subjects for experimentation (digging a hole, rolling logs), elements for construction (building a shelter or a pyramid), or objects of scientific investigation (worms and snakes).

John Dewey, the American philosopher and "father" of progressive education, emphasized the importance to children's growth of direct experience with raw materials. The "Dewey School" (the Laboratory School at the University of Chicago), which Dewey founded in 1896 with a group of colleagues, put into practice Dewey's theories. Classrooms at the school were provided with primary materials, such as sand, water, clay, and wood (for carpentry), as well as paper and paint. A book written some years later by two of the teachers at the school, articulates the rationale behind these choices:

> The child's impulse to do, to make—the constructive impulse—finds expression first in play, in rhythmic movement, in gesture, and make-believe; then becomes more definite and seeks outlet in shaping raw materials into tangible forms and permanent embodiment. (Mayhew & Edwards, 1936/1965, p. 40)

On the playground at the Mission Hill School, as we've seen, children took advantage of the many opportunities the environment provided to express their "constructive impulse[s]" in the ways suggested by the theory and practice at the Dewey School. The possibilities of making, shaping, transforming—of adding novelty to the scene—intrigued children at the end of the 20th century, just as they had a hundred years earlier.

INFLUENCE OF THE OBSERVER

A second explanation of why the sources of play were largely noncommercial might have had something to do with the observer, Beth. Beth was an influential figure on the playground, even when simply watching and making notes. Occasionally she actively participated in the ongoing scene—to contribute information, remind the children of basic playground rules, caution them about risky behavior, help settle arguments, comfort a child in distress, or join the children in play. The children, accepting her presence, were also curious about her note-taking.

> Again I was asked why I write everything down. "She's a research person," said Lizzie.

> I was asked by a 6-year-old why I wrote in a little book. When I told him it was so I could remember what children did and said, he commented, "You like doing that so you can learn about the world." And, indeed I do.

> A 6-year-old asked me, "Will you write that problem down?"

Beth, an experienced educator, was, in her words, "fascinated by the children's imaginative lives." On the playground, she responded particularly to their original, creative dramas as well as to their interest in the natural history of the playground. She herself was less informed about, and less interested in, TV and other commercial media. The kinds of activities, then, that particularly caught Beth's attention may have had some effect on the choices the children made—and how they played. They were probably aware of her reactions of interest and pleasure—or lack thereof.

VIOLENCE

Then, of course, there's the question of violence. Commercial media—films, TV, video games, and so on—are full of violence. The frequency of fights, battles, wars, murders, and the like has been well documented. Children react with terror, delight, fascination, excitement, and, in some cases, deep fear. Some become inured to scenes of violence—a reaction that may, in the long run, be more psychologically and socially damaging than fear. The school favored quieter modes, more thoughtful ways of responding to events—reflection, curiosity, empathy, and active imagining. Beth, as a responsible adult and representative of the school's authority, discouraged violent, unsafe, and aggressive behavior on the playground. Her comments, 8 years later:

> I did not think that sharp sticks were safe, so children invented less dangerous substitutes for guns and knives, pieces of bark, for

instance. Sometimes children went up to people and bang, banged. You could say I "censored," so the children turned to other games. They captured animals and put people in prison or cages but someone always rescued them. . . . Always when new children came in it was a surprise and sometimes a shock that [the children at Mission Hill] did not run around shouting and pushing and dragging.

Is there some benefit to children in acting out violent gestures in symbolic form (i.e., not literally dangerous), even if media-derived? If, as we've suggested, part of the function of dramatic play is to help children come to terms with the world around them and not be paralyzed by its mysteries and threats, then that includes the representation of violence. The children's lives are surrounded by violence, sometimes experienced at home or on the street, unavoidably seen or read about in the media. The basic question is whether Power Rangers and their ilk validate and thus encourage aggression or whether they provide some sense of safety or reassurance that the "good guys" will win out and protect society from evil.

SCHOOL VALUES

The educational values of the school as a whole reinforced those values, communicated, in one way or another, on the playground. Inside the building, in the classrooms and halls, there were notably few commercial materials to be seen. Children's work—paintings, models and constructions, graphs, writings, and so on—was everywhere, displayed on walls and tables (not "best work" but work representing whole groups), most having to do with the subject currently being studied. During the study of classical Greece, one might have seen in the hall a 6-foot-high ink drawing of an Ionic column; a carefully outlined and colored Greek alphabet; a group of illustrated essays on "My Favorite God"; a mounted museum photograph of the sculptured head of the goddess Diana; a series of drawings by second graders of "food from Greece"; photographs, taken by children, of Greek elements in local architecture; a colorfully painted, papier-mâché 3-D map of Greece; handwritten stories about Persephone and other gods and goddesses.

The teachers researched, found or created, organized and assembled the materials for the schoolwide curricular themes—ancient Greece, China, Egypt, and the Mayan civilization. Children, from kindergarten through grade 7, became engaged in the ancient culture through their active participation in finding out about, and representing, it. The themes, each of them rich in art and story, were so all-involving that it was not surprising to find them spilling over onto the playground. Greek heroes like Hercules or Achilles provided effective competition, at least in school, to Superman.

The usefulness of media-derived play depends on how much it is transformed, to what extent children adapt the figures and stories to their own psychic inclinations and needs. When playground dramas become repetitive, sterile, limited to scripts, their usefulness is minimal, perhaps even counterproductive. Transformed by children, media figures and dramas may serve almost as well as fairytales and myths. Godzilla and the Minotaur both represent evil power; both can be defeated by courageous heroes. Yet all schools have a responsibility, we believe, to advocate for quality and imagination, for cultural heritage and aesthetics. The media—powerful, glossy, and seductive—need no advocates. The schools and education do.

Epilogue: Wondering About the Future

The three of us—Beth, Brenda and Deborah—brought to the Mission Hill School over 200 years of lived experience in several U.S. cities and states and also abroad. Much of this experience had been part of the effort to reform schools for young children. We had worked mostly with relatively disadvantaged children—from low-income or unemployed families, often children of color, in rural, suburban, and urban settings.

The three of us held strikingly similar ideas about what young children needed most to thrive. Though we were occasionally at odds about particular practices, our disagreements were mostly useful to us and the school. Parents and even children at the school were sometimes unclear about our individual roles—the three Old Wise Ladies (OWLS) as we would jokingly define ourselves—or perhaps just three Old White Ladies.

Our impetus for writing this book was, most immediately, awareness of a growing national threat: the loss of play. The tragedy of such a deprivation for children and loss to public education was highlighted by the contrast to what we were observing at Mission Hill, where the value of play and the imagination were given time and space. The evidence is there, in "Notes from Outdoors." Children were demonstrating those remarkable qualities of thought that appear in many forms and are innate to humans almost from the moment of birth: speculation, imagination, and wonder ("'It's a clue . . . it's a raccoon. We found some grubs and I think raccoons eat grubs.'"; "Elizabeth held a piece of bark to her ear as she said, 'The robber is down there'").

By the time children arrive at school at age 3, 4, or 5, they have already accomplished wonders in a natural and efficient way. We once listed all the things children come to their first "public" settings already knowing and able to do. If we broke these pieces of knowledge and abilities into "teachable" units, they would constitute a curriculum that couldn't be "taught" in roughly a dozen years of formal schooling. But children have achieved all this more or less on their own initiative.

When they come to school, it's then the school's job—during those relatively few hours out of the children's days, weeks, and years when they are in the school's keeping—to continue the process of learning. How, then, do we school people plan for learning in this densely populated setting with few adults per child and in collaboration, one would hope, with those who are responsible for the children's out-of-school hours? How might we design the space itself, what might we add to it, and how might we divide up the time we have together?

We three OWLs, along with our colleagues, well understood that play was one important way in which young children both "work" and "learn." We agreed that children learn from the environment, from "things," and from their peers as well as from the adults whom they observe doing their adult things—cooking, cleaning, singing, reading aloud, and so on.

At the heart of the child's impulse to learn is speculation or wonder. In a chapter titled "Wonder as the Genesis of Knowledge," Edith Cobb (1977) writes that "the sense of wonder is spontaneous, a prerogative of childhood. When it is maintained as an attitude or point of view in later life . . . it incites the mind to organize novelty of pattern and form out of incoming information" (p. 27).

Wonder is the playful part of learning that sustains the potential for the future. "I wonder . . ." are the words of the speculative mind that characterizes a creative thinker. We might, at times, wish we could dispense with wondering because it can bring with it worries and fears. And it's fraught with risks: Will I be welcomed or rejected, will I be good at it or make a fool of myself? Speculating involves some physical and mental risks and requires being able, on some level, to trust one's own footing and the goodwill of others. For the young and inexperienced, it requires the situation to be sufficiently safe to go on playing another day.

Mission Hill's motto, adopted a few years after the school began, is WORK HARD AND BE KIND. "Play hard" might be just as valid, but it would be puzzling to many. "Work" and "play" are not in fact polar opposites, in spite of the common assumption. If "work" is defined as physical or mental effort, play can be hard work (as shown by the examples in Beth's columns). Children, playing along the "banks" of the blue plastic "Nile River" meandering down the hallway in the school, are inventing (or partially reinventing) a world. ("Watch out," yells a child, "a crocodile!" "I saw an asp," says another, peering into the blue "water.")

Is the wish for all children to be intellectuals pretentious and highfaluten? Or is it a reminder that all human beings are born as intellectuals, with their minds already hard at work figuring out the world within their reach. As that world expands and their reach encompasses more sources of knowledge (like books, movies, paintings), children's passion for knowing continues unless their life experiences make it difficult for learning to be rewarding, when some forms of learning become no fun, no longer playful work.

In the process of turning schools into competitive institutions, "racing to the top," we end up threatening the spirit of childhood. Because of our own limited histories and the generally accepted language around schooling—"grade level," "ahead or behind," "competent or proficient," "differentiated learning"—we begin to lose sight of what education means. These become the only words for describing children in school—children like those we observe playing in this book. "Knowing children well" becomes a matter of looking at test data.

Standardized tests are almost explicitly designed to underplay both intuition and imagination. Through years of training in seeking the "one-and-only" right answer, we've taught children to ignore the possibilities that so-called wrong answers embody. At a time in history when we are crying out for creative alternatives to seemingly intransigent problems, it may prove more perilous than we imagine to cut off at an early age the natural human tendency to seek alternatives, to imagine other viewpoints, to invent solutions that take into account the "wrong" but intriguing answers. Without being able to read the future, we suspect that early-childhood play and imagination may be more central to our viability as a species than current educational practice suggests.

Some degree of compliance and "standardization" (conforming to the standards of others) is, of course, part of growing up as members of society. However, in school, with the consent of children's families and communities, we can encourage children to continue playing: to imagine, to speculate about the world around them, to turn things upside down and around and envision new possibilities, to act as though we had infinite choices—and we might actually discover much that remains now hidden to us.

At the Mission Hill School, through Beth's weekly columns, we were able to recognize and honor a language different from that of the world of measurement and testing, a language that reflects a more interesting and convincing reality. The columns were a means of keeping all of us—staff, children, families, and the community—alert to what is important in schooling. Excerpts from the columns, put together here, reassure us, the authors, that we were acting as responsible custodians of childhood.

Mission Hill School, a Boston Pilot School

BEGINNINGS

Mission Hill School became part of the Boston public school system shortly after the Boston School Department and local teachers union agreed in 1995 to initiate "pilot schools"—an attempt, in part, to compete with the newly created state charter schools. Unlike charter schools, the pilots would still, to some degree, be under city control. A joint union/management committee approved proposals for the pilot schools on the basis of how they proposed to make use of the extraordinary freedom they would have from both city and union rules and regulations (not ultimately from state authority, however). The major exceptions to this freedom were wages and benefits, still to be set by the union.

The new schools were mandated to set up their own governing systems in collaboration with the School Department and union, according to a presumed basic understanding. A group of distinguished local educators, in addition to the three authors of this book, began working in the fall of 1996 on plans for the new pilot school. Our proposal was accepted soon after, and we spent the following winter and spring working out the practical details.

The last task of the planning committee, after designating Deborah Meier as principal, was to hire staff. Committee members fanned out, observing and interviewing candidates for the teaching positions: two K/1 teachers, two 2/3 teachers, and one 4/5 teacher. The five teachers we hired were experienced (though not in the Boston schools); most had some background in progressive-minded practices. We also hired a half-time administrative assistant, an assistant to the principal, and five interns. A group of unpaid student teachers and volunteers supplemented the regular staff and the School Department contributed a custodian, a part-time special education consultant, and a part-time nurse. A further staff person helped the principal respond to external demands, served as a development "officer" for the school, and eventually built a strong community service program.

The school opened in the fall of 1997. From the start, we worked with several colleges, forming close ties with Wheelock College and, over the years, with Lesley University, Northeastern University, and Tufts University, all of which sent us student teachers. Mission Hill School was also part of two networks: the Boston Pilot Schools (most of them high schools) and the Coalition of Essential Schools, a national network led by the prominent educator Ted Sizer. In Boston, the Center for Collaborative Education, an independent not-for-profit agency, supported both these networks. The Center was useful in helping the pilot schools negotiate difficulties between the School Department's original intent of providing them with more autonomy and interpretation of those intentions in actual practice. For example, while Mission Hill School was part of the regular lottery system for student assignment, the Boston School Department and the Boston Teachers Union agreed that families would have to visit the school before being accepted, to ensure that they were well informed about our practices. The final choice, however, lay with families who were selected by the lottery (with the exception of siblings of current or previously enrolled students and the children of staff, who had automatic priority). It took some time to be sure that this agreement was well understood and was actually put into operation. Also, issues arose over our voice in the selection of school department personnel assigned to the building—the part-time nurse, custodian, special education specialist, and so on. It was important that these individuals to some extent shared the school's philosophy—that their behavior and ways of relating to children, for instance, were not radically different from those of the regular staff. These issues have never been completely resolved.

The powers of the Board—five members selected by parents, five by staff, and five chosen as community representatives by both parents and staff (later students were added)—were not clear: Who really got to hire and fire the principal? In its early days, the school faced other big questions, too. It was designed as a citywide option, but was this decision one that the School Department could later change? How might the state and federal government's increasing involvement in curriculum and assessment affect Mission Hill School? Similarly, the original proposal for the school planned for faculty decision making on most educational matters, but the details of such governance were always contestable and contested. Also, the principal, as essentially lead-teacher, was critical to the design, and that, too, had always been a fragile concept, given the educational surround that saw principals as chief monitors and "deciders."

Thus, from the start, the school was dealing locally with many aspects of school reform at a stressful moment in its overall history—from the pedagogical, curricular, cultural, and regulatory details of running a school with eventually about 175 students, to its connection to other pilots, the Boston School Department, the Boston Teachers Union, and the broader areas of policy.

Mission Hill School was, and still is, trying to carry out its mission in the midst of an often unsympathetic, at times resentful, educational environment. This book makes a case relevant to one of the most important areas of potential misunderstanding: the school's active commitment to the value of play and the life of the imagination.

THE NEIGHBORHOOD

Roxbury is an economically and racially mixed urban area. The original residents of Alleghany Street, on which the school faces, were German immigrants who worked as supervisors in nearby breweries. The area was populated from the mid-19th century on by successive waves of immigrants—predominantly Irish, Jewish, and, in the mid-20th century, African American (most of the latter having migrated from the South). More recently, a significant number of Hispanics have added to the mix, although African Americans still constitute over half of the population.

The large, impressive Mission Church, which gave its name to the hill and surrounding area, dominates the nearby blocks on Tremont Street. At a short distance are a number of institutions of higher education, among them Northeastern University, Wentworth Academy, Roxbury Community College, the Massachusetts College of Art, the Massachusetts College of Pharmacy, and the Harvard Medical School. The Boston Museum of Fine Arts and the Gardner Museum are within an easy 20-minute walk. The immediate surroundings of the school, though, on Mission Hill, are mostly residential properties—largely frame houses, many with multiple occupancy.

THE DEMOGRAPHICS

The Mission Hill School opened in the fall of 1997 with 104 children— 55 boys and 49 girls—in grades K–5. The population was diverse in terms of both race and economic status: The children were classified as 43% Black, 30% White, 22% Hispanic, and 5% Asian (though a number were actually of mixed parentage). About half of the families were low income, an estimate based on eligibility for free or reduced-fee lunch. In short, the population reflected that of the Boston public schools. Over 80% of the children came from the communities of Dorchester, Jamaica Plain, and

Roxbury; the rest were from Hyde Park, Roslindale, Brighton, and Boston proper.

Of the seven original core staff (teachers and administrators), four were White, two Black, and one Hispanic. In subsequent years, as the school grew (eventually to include grades K–8), the demographics continued to reflect the population of the Boston schools. The number of staff increased as well, its composition remaining more or less consistently a third to a half persons of color.

The Mission Hill Newsletter

MISSION HILL SCHOOL **NEWS**

Week of April 10, 2000   Vol. 3, No. 31

REMINDERS

• **Tuesday, April 11:**
East House family night and open house, 5:45 p.m.

• **Thursday, April 13:**
Violin & viola classes meet today instead of Friday this week.

• **April 17–21:**
SCHOOL VACATION WEEK.

• **Wednesday, April 26:**
Parent Council meeting, 6:30–8:00 p.m.

• **Thursday, April 27:**
Alvin Ailey Dance Company performance, 12 noon (whole school).

THERE IS A PLACE

There is a place away from
home away from cities and
tall buildings. A place that is
peaceful and full of joy.
There is a place where animals roam
a place full of harmony.
There is a place
that is almost perfect for me.
There is a place in the town of Athol
that place full of joy
the Farm School.   —*Kin Moy*

ACROSTIC POEM

Fun thing at the Farm School.
Animals are great there.
Running calf.
Mooing cows every day.

Soft little calves.
Cute calves and cows.
Hairy pigs.
Oinking pigs.
Oh the wind is nice.
Low the cows go.   —*Chantel O'Bryant*

LETTER FROM MISSION HILL

The Hurried, Uncaring Child

Dear Families, Students, Staff, and Friends,

I spent April Fool's Day in New York City with hundreds of colleagues discussing the testing mania that is sweeping the nation. What we need is a real offensive against bad schooling and destructive education. Instead we are focused on preparing kids for tests.

Quite aside from the usual big dangers it poses—the centralization of authority, the massive failure of large numbers of our most underserved children, and the dumbing down of curriculum in many of our best schools—it also actually maims. The newspapers have reported several cases of suicide and mental breakdown linked to high-pressure testing that seeks to cram more and more information into every student.

We're asking kids to "know" stuff it would take, the experts tell us, nine more years of schooling just to cover. How to do this? Work faster, work harder, work longer hours. Cut recess, cut field trips, cut birthday parties, cut the frills.

Peter Steinfels, the *New York Times* religion and ethics columnist and former editor of *Commonweal* magazine (a Catholic weekly), raises another interesting argument against this dangerous increase in pressure on our kids. His point isn't about testing, but it nevertheless applies. We are preparing children to work hard, but not to think, imagine, understand, or—here's the new wrinkle—care.

Describing an experiment conducted some years ago at Princeton Theological Seminary, Steinfels suggests that Good Samaritans are people who are not in a hurry—that is, people with the leisure to stop and attend to others. The more rushed we are, the less likely we are to respond to the needy. So, he says, what lies ahead?

The average married couple with children now collectively puts in eight more work weeks every year than they did in 1979. They spend, he reports, 22 fewer hours weekly with their children than in 1969.

As we contemplate summer plans for Mission Hillers, we too worry whether to recommend summer school or wonderful camping experiences—pressed as we are to help kids "raise

As we press kids to work harder, can we expect them to do fewer good deeds?

scores." In the long run (and maybe even in the short run), a great summer camp will do more for academic success than five more weeks of schoolwork. But dare we encourage youngsters to take the time, to explore, inquire, imagine, play? And care?

If our children are raised increasingly in institutions focused on their production of ever more speeded-up work, and fewer opportunities for leisure and thoughtfulness, can we expect fewer of them to do good deeds? Is the price remotely worth it? Will we wake up in time to get off this treadmill?

I keep hoping it's just an April Fool's joke.   —*Deborah Meier*

The Mission Hill School is a pilot school of the Boston Public Schools

Thomas Payzant, Superintendent
Deborah Meier, Principal
Brian Straughter, Assistant Principal

67 Alleghany Street
Roxbury, MA 02120
Main Office: 617.635.6384

HOT TOPICS

Science as a Paradigm for Life

At the Mission Hill School we're strong believers in the value of scientific inquiry. Our five habits of mind are grounded in respect for science. But there are dangers in the dominant view of science that ruled our world for many years, and which is less dominant today in the "hard" sciences but still holds sway in the "soft" ones—like education.

The statements below come from the work of the late Isaiah Berlin, a noted philosopher and student of the history of science. They speak to us powerfully about some of our most mundane concerns.

"The scientific 'paradigm' which dominated the century, with its strong implication that only that which was quantifiable, or at any rate measurable—that to which in principle mathematical methods were applicable—was real, strongly reinforced the old conviction that to every question there was only one true answer.... To impose such a belief must always lead to persecution and deprivation of liberty."

"Freedom to err," Berlin argued, is more important than holding "correct opinions."

Women Artists of Color

Our own Ayla Gavins is among the artists whose work is currently on exhibit at the Harriet Tubman Gallery at 566 Columbus Avenue, at the corner of Massachusetts Avenue. The exhibit is sponsored by NEWOCA, an organization for women artists of color from New England. There will be a reception for the artists this Friday from 5 to 8 p.m. For more information call 375-8133. Regular gallery hours are 9 a.m. to 8 p.m. Monday through Friday and 10 a.m. to 2 p.m. Saturdays.

Coming Soon

An outline of our first trial framework for the study of the visual arts and science will be available in a few weeks. And a shorter, more user-friendly guide to our math curriculum will also be available this spring. We're doing this in collaboration with other pilot schools, so it has taken longer (but will be stronger) than we anticipated.

World Languages

Our sixth- and seventh-graders are formally studying French or Spanish, thanks to Heidi Lyne, Priscilla Aquino, Lizette van Leuven, Thomas Archer, Heydi Foster, and some of our students who speak other languages, too. It's going well. We are planning to continue this program next year, and beyond.

In the lower grades we are introducing, rather informally, some experiences with languages other than English, mostly Spanish. But this depends a lot on the skills of each teacher and assistant, and the particular focus of the curriculum. (Right now, learning Chinese seems more relevant.)

We're enjoying it. Thanks also to the parents who've been pushing us to do more of this.

Helping Kids with Math

Try helping your kids at home by substituting small simple numbers for big complicated ones when they get stumped. Example: I often forget how to multiply or divide fractions. If faced with $3/8 \times 7/15$, I feel lost for a moment. I try to remember how you are supposed to proceed. But when this happens I go back to "What's half of a half?" Aha: one-fourth. So $1/2 \times 1/2 = 1/4$. Therefore, the answer is to multiply the tops and multiply the bottoms. So $3/8 \times 7/15 = 21/120$.

Once I remember what I'm really doing—and simple numbers make it easier to focus on understanding the task—the procedure for solving it falls into place.

Another example: If 1845 students are distributed into 123 classrooms so that each has the same number of students, how many will be in each class? I'm intimidated by those numbers before I finish the sentence. But if I switch it to 100 students in 4 classrooms, I know right away how to solve it: divide 100 by 4. Then I go back to the original problem with confidence: $1845 \div 123 = 15$.

Try this with some of your child's homework problems. If it works, let me know! (In real life, alas, we each have tricks that help us but are hard to pass on to others. Does this help anyone out there?) —*Deborah Meier*

⋅⋅News from⋅⋅ ⋅⋅Outdoors⋅⋅

SOME CHILDREN FOUND a garter snake last week. No one screamed with fear this year. Looking at the daffodils through the fence, a five-year-old said, "They're popping up." *And digging in the hole is back.*

"The water level was up to here," said a boy, pointing to the top line on the side of the hole. Lukas needed some dirt so three children filled some boxes for him, conversing as they dug:

"We need a world dictionary. We need to find out all about things. This is dirt. It's part earth, rocks, and dead things."

"I found a crystal rock. Maybe it's a baby of the big one we took inside last year."

Older children at the second playtime took all the rocks and logs out of the hole and began to dig the hole deeper. A group of younger children put a plank against the wall and carried mud from the hole to cover the plank.

"We need to feed the elephant. We need grass."

The same group of children who played family games last week continued their roles in the lilac trees and around the big tree.

"I'll lock the doors."

"I'm strong. I took the money."

"Use your powers, girl."

The West House planted a ginko tree and a flowering cherry tree in front of the school. A group of sixth graders are making a raised garden in hopes of growing some Chinese vegetables.

—*Beth Lerman*

Mission Hill School News

Published every Monday during the school year for the parents, students, staff, and friends of the Mission Hill School, 67 Alleghany St., Roxbury, Mass. 02120.

Principal: Deborah Meier
Coordinator: Helen Fouhey, 541-3899
Editor: Ed Miller, 492-5684

Copy Deadline: All news items and other submissions should be typed or neatly printed, signed, and put in Ed Miller's box in the main office by 10 a.m. Thursday.

References

Armstrong, M. (2009, June). The pedagogy of the imagination. *Learning Landscapes, 2,* 48.

Carlsson-Paige, N. (2008). *Taking back childhood.* New York: Hudson Street Press.

Cobb, E. (1977). *The ecology of imagination in childhood.* New York: Columbia University Press.

Freud, S. (1961). *Civilization and its discontents* (J. Riviere, Trans.). In J. Strachey (Ed.), *The standard edition of the complete psychological works of Sigmund Freud* (Vol. 20). London: Hogarth Press. (Original work published 1930)

Mayhew, K. C., & Edwards, A. C. (1965). *The Dewey school: The Laboratory School of the University of Chicago, 1896–1903.* New York: Appleton-Century. (Original work published 1936)

Further Reading

Armstrong, M. (1980). *Closely observed children*. London: Writers and Readers in Association with Chameleon Press.

Chudacoff, H. (2007). *Children at play: An American history*. New York: New York University Press.

Duckworth, E. (1987). *The having of wonderful ideas*. New York: Teachers College Press.

Ekind, D. (1981). *The hurried child*. Reading, MA: Addison-Wesley Publishing.

Engel, B. (1995). *Considering children's art*. Washington, DC: National Association for the Education of Young Children.

Hawkins, D. (1974). *The informed vision, essays on learning and human nature*. New York: Agathon Press.

Hirsh-Pasek, K., Michnick Golinkoff, R., Berk, L., & Singer, D. (2009). *A mandate for playful learning in preschools*. New York: Oxford University Press.

Linn, S. (2008). *The case for make believe*. New York: The New Press.

Meier, D. (1995). *The power of their ideas*. Boston: Beacon Press.

Meier, D. (2002). *In schools we trust*. Boston: Beacon Press.

Middlebrooks, S. (1998). *Getting to know city kids*. New York: Teachers College Press.

Mintz, S. (2004). *Huck's raft*. Cambridge, MA: Harvard University Press.

Opie, I., & Opie, P. (1969). *Children's games in street and playground*. Oxford, England: Oxford University Press.

Paley, V. G. (1981). *Wally's stories*. Cambridge, MA: Harvard University Press.

Paley, V. G. (2004). *A Child's Work: The importance of fantasy play*. Chicago: University of Chicago Press.

Polakow, V. (1982). *The erosion of childhood*. Chicago: University of Chicago Press.

Vygotsky, V. S. (1978). *Mind in society*. Cambridge, MA: Harvard University Press.

Weber, L., & Alberty, B. (1997). *Looking back and thinking forward*. New York: Teachers College Press.

Winnicott, D. W. (1971). *Playing and reality*. London: Tavistock Publications.

Index

Note: The letter f indicates a figure.

Absences, as family play concept, 22
Acting out
  as playground problem, 10
  in symbolic form, benefits
    of, 102
Administrative positions, 109, 112
Adults
  influence on play choice, 86–87
  playground memories of, 43
Age, and gender issues, 91–95
Aliens, chasing games with, 26–28
Ambiguity, in "good" vs. "bad" character
    roles, 29
Amphibians, in playground, 5, 47
Ancient civilizations curriculum, 57–64
Animal families, as play concept, 22–25
Animals. *See also* Creatures
  appeal of, 25
  children playing as, 22–25, 23f, 47
  as source of play, 44–48
Anthropomorphism, 22–25, 23f, 47
Anticipation, digging activity and, 41
Areas of play. *See* Content of play
Armstrong, Michael, "The Pedagogy of the
    Imagination," 63
Authority, students exercising, 8
Auxiliary staff positions, 110

"Bad" guy character, 98
  chasing games and, 26–28
  cultural lore and, 73
  role ambiguity and, 29
Ball games, wall for, 4–5
  wall ball, 82
Basketball, 6, 7

"Basketball" (writing assignment), 93
Batman, 99
Beech tree, in playground, 3–4, 4f
  as "castle," 15, 16
  as "house," 13–14
Blind man's bluff, 82
Boston Museum of Fine Arts, 111
Boston Pilot Schools network, 110
Boston public school (BPS) system, "pilot
    school" application to, ix
Boston School Department, 110, 111
Boston Teachers Union, 110, 111
Boys
  and gender roles, 91
  mimicking sports figures, 80–81
BPS (Boston public school) system, "pilot
    school" application to, ix
Butterflies, in playground, 47–48

"Car crashes," as play concept, 21
Carlsson-Paige, Nancy. *Taking Back
    Childhood,* 97
Castle(s)
  beech tree as, 15, 16
  as play concept, 16
Catastrophes, as play concept, 29–31
Catching games, 26–29
Catchment area, for school, 111–112
Center for Collaborative Education, 110
Central Park East, New York City, ix
Chants, 82–83
  risqué, 95–96
Charter schools, "pilot schools" vs., 109
Chasing games, 7, 26–29, 88
  problems with, 75

119

About the Authors

DEBORAH MEIER has spent almost five decades working in public education as a teacher, writer, and public advocate. Beginning her teaching career as a kindergarten and Head Start teacher in Chicago, Philadelphia, and, in 1974, New York, she became the founder and director of Central Park East School, a small, progressive public school in New York City. Meier went on to help establish a network of small NYC schools. In 1996 she founded the Mission Hill Public School in Boston. Deborah Meier has written numerous articles and several books on educational matters and has received honorary degrees from more than a dozen colleges and universities, as well as a MacArthur Fellowship, in recognition of her work on behalf of schoolchildren. She is currently a Senior Scholar on the faculty of the Steinhardt School of Education at New York University.

BRENDA S. ENGEL began her career as an elementary school art teacher and has written about, lectured and given workshops on children's art. As a faculty member at Lesley College (now Lesley University) she taught and practiced qualitative program evaluation, mainly in the field of education. Since her retirement in 1992, Brenda Engel has given time to tutoring children in various public school settings, one of which was the Mission Hill School in Boston, the venue of this book. A lifelong watercolorist, she exhibits work in the New England area.

BETH TAYLOR, after graduating from college, went to England, where she taught in an elementary school and later became head of a state primary (elementary) school. In England, and then back in the States, her work has spanned pre-school through college, including teacher training, program evaluation, early childhood education, and teaching at the Mission Hill School in Boston. Her observations of children on the playground, written for the Mission Hill School newsletter, provide the backbone for this book. She lives in Lincoln, Massachusetts, with her husband, who is also a teacher.